Introduction

As the only magazine focusing on literature for adolescents and their librarians, *VOYA*'s young adult book reviews have helped build young adult library collections since 1978. Many young adult librarians rely on *VOYA*'s reviews as their main resource for book selection.

VOYA's reviewers are librarians, professors, and teachers with expertise in young adult literature and experience working with teens. There are currently one hundred ninety adult reviewers. Their average length of reviewing service is about twelve years, although some have been with us for more than twenty years. *VOYA* has welcomed teen reviewers for many years and has an average of thirty-five teen reviewers at any one time. Teen reviewers are partnered with adult reviewers so that teen input complements several of the adult reviews in every issue. Our review editor, Lisa Kurdyla, communicates with all of our reviewers, interviewing them to determine the kinds of books that are a good match for each reviewer, and working with them as needed through the reviewing process.

The unique Q (quality) and P (popularity) rating system has been an important tool to help busy young adult librarians make their purchase and reading selections. The original rating system was adapted by Dorothy M. Broderick from a small music newsletter no longer in publication. The Q rating is strictly a 1 to 5 rating with 1 being the worst and 5 being the best, while the P rating is more subjective to the segment of the teen audience the book is meant to target. As you can see in the table below, a 5Q 2P book could be a very good book for a particular audience of teen readers. A 5Q 3P book may be a very good book but it needs help off the shelf.

Quality

5Q	Hard to imagine it being better written.
4Q	Better than most, marred by occasional lapses.
3Q	Readable, without serious defects.
2Q	Better editing or work by the author might have warranted a 3Q.
1Q	Hard to understand how it got published, except in relation to its P rating (and not even then sometimes).

Popularity

5P   Every YA (who reads) was dying to read it yesterday.

4P   Broad general or genre YA appeal.

3P   Will appeal with pushing.

2P   For the YA reader with a special interest in the subject.

1P   No teen will read unless forced to for assignments.

The reviewers also rate the books for recommended grades: M for middle school, J for junior high, S for senior high, and A/YA which is an adult book with young adult appeal. The middle school rating was not part of the original rating system and was added later. Other notations included in this compilation include NF for nonfiction; GN for graphic novel; and SF/F/H for science fiction, fantasy, and horror; genres that have been of particular interest to teens.

Additionally, major book awards were added to this list of titles to see which of our reviewers' best books went on to find recognition elsewhere. Among the awards seen here are: Michael L. Printz, John Newbery, Coretta Scott King, Best Books for Young Adults, Quick Picks for Young Adults, Teens' Top Ten, Popular Paperbacks for Young Adults, Guardian Award, Carnegie Medal, Best Fiction for Young Adults, Mythopoeic Fantasy Award, USA Today Bestseller, Nonfiction Award, Morris Award, and the Edgar Award. Many of these titles have stood the test of time and some have lived their lives, but all were well-loved by our reviewers when first read.

From 2000 through 2012, *VOYA* reviewed 14,545 books for young adults and their librarians. According to *Library and Book Trade Almanac,* the number of publications for young adults grew during 2005 to 2007 and has seen a gradual decline in the following years. Over this decade we saw growing trends in glbtq titles, books with paranormal themes—such as vampires, werewolves, angels, demons and zombies—and more multicultural main characters and settings.

Our office receives an average of four hundred books per month, with the largest number arriving in February, March, and April. Currently, about one hundred ninety of those get reviewed. Titles that are not reviewed may be additional volumes of series nonfiction and we now review those series once a year. Other reasons some titles may not get reviewed include: they are not published for young adults, they have limited or no young adult appeal, or they were sent to us too long after publication. Out of those reviewed titles, slightly over one percent, or one hundred fifty-six, were what we call Perfect Tens, having received a 5Q *and* 5P rating.

We hope this list is helpful to you as a collection development tool, a weeding tool, a research tool, a reading guide, and as general interest in good young adult literature.

—RoseMary Honnold, *VOYA* Editor-in-Chief

"Ask the Librarian." American Libraries. *http://americanlibrariesmagazine.org/ask-ala-librarian/number-childrens-books-published*

VOYA's Review Codes

Quality

5Q	Hard to imagine it being better written.
4Q	Better than most, marred by occasional lapses.
3Q	Readable, without serious defects.
2Q	Better editing or work by the author might have warranted a 3Q.
1Q	Hard to understand how it got published, except in relation to its P rating (and not even then sometimes).

Popularity

5P	Every YA (who reads) was dying to read it yesterday.
4P	Broad general or genre YA appeal.
3P	Will appeal with pushing.
2P	For the YA reader with a special interest in the subject.
1P	No teen will read unless forced to for assignments.

Grade Level Interest

M	Middle School (defined as grades 6-8).
J	Junior High (defined as grades 7-9).
S	Senior High (defined as grades 10-12).
A/YA	Adult-marketed book recommended for teens.

Format/Genre

GN	Graphic Novel Format
SF/F/H	Science Fiction/Fantasy/Horror
NF	Nonfiction

Acampora, Paul. **Defining Dulcie**. Speak, 2008, ©2006. 176p. $6.99 pb. 978-0-14-241183-4.
VOYA April 2006. **5Q · 5 · M · J · S**
Popular Paperbacks for Young Adults 2009.

If sixteen-year-old Dulcie Jones were making a movie of her life, she would cast Harrison Ford as her father-and rewrite the screenplay so that Ford would live. Dulcie's life is not a film, and her father does not survive, but her life moves on. Following her father's funeral, Dulcie and her mother relocate to California, where Dulcie feels disconnected from her New England roots. Even after weeks gazing at San Francisco Bay, Dulcie misses home, so when her mother makes plans to sell her father's '68 Chevy pickup, Dulcie makes her own bold move. Stealing the truck, she drives back to Connecticut to live with her grandfather and return to her job as his student janitor at the local high school. Dulcie finds unexpected friendship upon returning, and the bond that she forms with her new coworker, Roxanne Soule, redefines both their lives when Roxanne leaves her abusive home.

Acampora's first novel is a splendidly unpretentious story about the resiliency of the human spirit. It is a consummate blend of clever dialogue and engaging narrative peppered with Dulcie's hilarious and heartwarming reminiscences about the places she visits on her cross-country journey. Acampora's work strikes a perfect balance between the serious and the comical. His strong and delightfully human characters are sure to appeal across gender lines. Recommended for skilled and reluctant readers ages ten and up, Dulcie's story will particularly appeal to those who enjoy reading Joan Bauer, Sharon Creech, and Richard Peck. Make room for Dulcie on your bookshelves now.—Sherry Korthals.

Alender, Katie. **As Dead as It Gets: Bad Girls Don't Die**. Hyperion, 2012. 448p. $16.99. 978-1-4231-3472-5.
VOYA August 2012. **5Q · 5P · J · S**

Two and a half months after Lydia's funeral, sixteen-year-old Alexis feels more lost and alone than ever. Being kept at a distance by the kids at school is painful, and having Carter break up with her hurts more, but maybe worst of all is being afraid to look through the viewfinder of her beloved camera. Now Alexis cannot look at a photograph without seeing ghostly images of the dead and how they died. When Jared, a cute boy she met during a photo contest in September, begins to show interest, Alexis is hesitant but hopeful: but nothing is that easy for Alexis. When girls start to disappear, all connected in some way to her new relationship, Alexis realizes there is a new spirit in town, and it is angry.

Delivering even more fabulously unforgettable, spine-tingling moments, this third entry in the *Bad Girls Don't Die* series upholds the high standards of superbly crafted storytelling set twice before. Just when it seems the characters might be falling into a caricature trap, they break free and become real again. The complex supernatural details and developing personal relationships are nicely balanced to keep readers turning the pages with anticipation. In the tradition of all excellent scary movies, fans might just find themselves repeatedly shouting, "Don't do it!" in hopes of warning Alexis, but lucky for the reader, she never seems to hear. This is not a choice for the faint of heart or for those who object to stories centered around witchcraft or the occult.—Stacey Hayman.

Anderson, Laurie Halse. **Twisted**. Viking, 2007. 256p. $16.99. 978-0-670-06101-3. $9.99 pb. 978-0-14-241184-1. PLB $18.99. 978-1-4395-1066-7.
VOYA April 2007. **5Q · 5P · S**
ALA Best Books for Young Adults 2008.
ALA Quick Pick for Young Adults 2008.
Teens' Top Ten 2008.
Popular Paperbacks for Young Adults 2012.

In the universe of high school, Tyler Miller used to be invisible. Completely average and on the nerdy side, Tyler went unnoticed by everyone except the occasional bully. But things are different since he was arrested for doing graffiti and sentenced to community service. Tyler's physique is changed by a summer of hard labor, and he is suddenly noticed by Bethany Milbury, the most popular of popular girls. And by the daughter of his workaholic father's boss. And by the sister of Tyler's worst enemy. Tyler's world changes as he struggles with the new roles he finds himself in at home and at school. His new physical strength brings new responsibilities. He soon finds that reputation is sometimes stronger than action and that doing the right thing is not always easy or even clear.

Tyler's voice in turn is rich with humor, rage, and despair. Anderson again presents readers with a sympathetic protagonist surrounded by a deftly drawn cast of characters. Tyler's relationships with the people in his life are authentically depicted. His interactions with his dysfunctional family and computer-geek best friend are particularly well drawn. Tyler faces issues that are both universal and original, from overwhelming lust and an overloaded school schedule to complex notions of manhood. The way he handles himself will have readers both cringing and cheering. This compelling novel of growth and maturity will be eagerly received by readers awaiting another story from this talented author.—Heather Pittman.

Anhalt, Ariela. **Freefall**. Houghton Mifflin Harcourt, 2009. 256p. $17. 978-0-15-206567-6. $7.99 pb. 978-0-547-55216-3.
VOYA October 2009. **5Q · 5P · J · S**

Truth is a relative experience. Sometimes vantage point is the deciding factor in whether something is true. No one knows this fact better than Luke. He witnessed a fatal fall that left a new member of his school's fencing team dead. Problem is, it was his best friend's hand that gave the fatal push to the boy who died on the rocks below a cliff. Luke is torn. Hayden is the popular kid who has given Luke a name among their peers. Hayden exudes wealth and all the trappings, but more important, Hayden is someone who cared about Luke when he had no one. Then along comes Russell—the new kid with something to prove—and he is locked in a bitter war with Hayden. What is Luke to do? He does not care for Russell, but he is not so confident that Hayden is doing the right thing by making Russell's life at Briar Academy less than stellar. Luke is ill prepared for the events that spiral downward leading to Russell's death. He is even less prepared to be launched into a case being built against his best friend. Readers will wonder right up until the end if Luke will do the right thing and even call to question what is the right thing from Luke's perspective.

Teens will love this title because it is full of page-turning events and is difficult to put down. It is an essential purchase for any public or school library that serves teens. —Robbie L. Flowers.

Ashton, Brodi. **Everbound: An Everneath Novel**. Balzer + Bray/HarperCollins, 2013. 368p. $17.99. 978-0-06-207116-3.
VOYA December 2012. **5Q · 5P · M · J · S**

With Jack trapped in the Everneath, Nikki tries to reconstruct the pieces of her borrowed life—the life Jack restored to her at the sacrifice of his own. Yet every night, Jack appears in her dreams, clinging to Nikki during the Feed as she clung to him but he is growing weaker. Nikki vows to free Jack, but Cole foils her first trip to the Everneath. She persists, finally threatening Cole with her own annihilation if he will not help her. She, Max, and Cole begin a perilous journey through the circles of hell in constant fear of discovery by the queen. They reach the Tunnels, but as Nikki tries to dig Jack out, Cole "kicks" her to the surface. Inexplicably, Jack returns but has changed physically, and Nikki discovers that she has lost her earthly heart.

The Everneath comes to life in lurid descriptions of the circles of hell, weaving literary and mythological references into the mix. Ashton's vivid images of the hands of the Forfeits reaching out of the earth are chilling. Subtle but solid character development makes Nikki's and Cole's actions ring true. Nikki's dogged determination to rescue Jack clouds her judgment. She demands help from the only person who can enter the Everneath while keeping her concealed. Through clever manipulation, Cole's real motives for helping Nikki are concealed until the final page. The surprise ending will leave stunned fans pleading for more. This worthy successor to **Everneath** (Balzer + Bray, 2012/**VOYA** December 2011) will be in high demand. Libraries are advised to buy more than one copy.—Nancy Wallace.

_____. **Everneath**. Balzer + Bray/HarperCollins, 2012. 384p. $17.99. 978-0-06-207113-2.
VOYA December 2011. **5Q · 5P · J · S**

For one hundred years, Nikki lay cocooned in the Everneath, in the arms of Cole, an Everliving, who fed on her emotions to stay alive. Now the Feed is over, and Nikki returns to the ruins of her former life. In Nikki's hometown, only six months have passed since her disappearance. Now she must make excuses to her father, her friends, and her boyfriend, Jack, to explain where she has been. She has six months to say goodbye to everyone she loves before the Everneath swallows her up forever, six desperate months to hope and pray that somehow there is a solution other than complete oblivion.

The author brings a fresh, innovative concept to young adult fiction with well-developed characters and a fantastic plot line. Everlivings feed on emotions. Cole's rock band feeds on its audience's emotional high, collecting eager fans. They can ease pain, loneliness, and grief. They prey on humans in their weakest moments and then destroy their lives forever. After a misunderstanding with Jack, Nikki is sucked into the underworld by Cole's promise of comfort and finds only emptiness instead. And yet it is Jack's love that sustains her through the endless Feed and eventually saves her. Mythology is skillfully interwoven with current culture as Nikki's experience parallels the story of Persephone. This exceptional love story has no happy ending: Jack sacrifices his own life for Nikki to survive. Libraries are advised to buy multiple copies—this one will fly off the shelves!—Nancy Wallace.

Bacigalupi, Paolo. **The Drowned Cities**. Little, Brown, 2012. 448p. $17.99. 978-0-316-20037-0.
VOYA April 2012. **5Q · 5P · J · S** (SF/H/F)
    In the future, the water levels have risen enough to "drown" urban coastal areas of what was once the United States of America. China has come attempting to bring order to this lawless area. The Chinese bring with them genetically-engineered dog soldiers designed to fight to the death for their master. Tool is one such solider. When attempting to escape from warlords, he is gravely injured in a fight with a giant crocodile. Thinking he might be good food, war maggots, Mahlia and Mouse, come upon him. Tool attacks and takes Mouse hostage in exchange for Mahlia's medical help. Mahlia goes back to the doctors with whom she is staying only to find out that they are now housing the soldiers who are looking for Tool. Since she is part Chinese, the soldiers look for a way to hurt Mahlia. In her diversion to escape with medicine to help Tool and save Mouse, many soldiers are wounded or killed causing them to retaliate and kill most of the village in which they were staying. Mouse attempts to save the doctor and is forced to enlist in the group. Mahlia feels awful for running and decides to take Tool and save Mouse. She must fight her way through the Drowned Cities with Tool to save Mouse from the war and himself.
    Bacigalupi brings to life a post-apocalyptic America that thrills the mind. Never would we imagine that China would have to save us from our own destruction. Just like Frankenstein's monster, Tool is shown to be more human and civilized than any of the ruthless human characters in the story.—Barbara Allen.

Backpack Books. DK, 2002. 192p. Trade pb. Glossary. Illus. Photos.
    VOYA October 2002. **5Q · 5P · M · J · S** (NF)
Clark, Neil, and William Lindsay, with additional material from Dougal Dixon. **1001 Facts About Dinosaurs**. 978-0-7894-8448-2.
    O.P.
Stott, Carole, and Clint Twist. **1001 Facts About Space**. 978-0-7894-8450-5.
    O.P.
    A human walking on the "extremely hostile" surface of Venus would surely be toast-and flat toast at that. The planet's temperature stays close to 896 degrees Fahrenheit, thanks to the thick blanket of fluffy sulfuric acid clouds and the surface pressure, which is ninety times that of Earth's at sea level. These frightening facts are typical of the information found in books in this series. **Dinosaurs** warns that any creature caught walking on Earth's surface during the Cretaceous Period might come face to face with one of the many species of Dromaeosaurids, swift, intelligent carnivores with stereoscopic vision,

razor sharp teeth, and long, slicing talons, which were used to cut three-foot-long gashes in their prey before devouring them alive. The typical middle or elementary school student taking in these two books is likely to think, "Cool!" Both texts tend to leave out boring details and stick to the interesting ones, starting with overall explanations of their topics, before becoming progressively more specific. **Space** moves in from the outer galaxies, finally examining Earth's solar system and human attempts to explore space. **Dinosaurs** begins with general discussions of the three periods when dinosaurs ruled the Earth, covering 160 million years before talking about how man discovered the fossil record, and finally giving specific, detailed descriptions of individual dinosaur species.

Both books have a wealth of illustrations. Those in **Dinosaurs** comprise a nice balance between photographs of actual fossilized skeletons, artists' renderings, and three-dimensional models. The quality of color and clarity of detail is as good as most other dinosaur books and on a par with much more expensive ones. Of similar quality, the illustrations in **Space** include artists' renderings, three-dimensional models, and photographs. Both books have large reference sections that include quick facts organized in an almanac-style arrangement. The reference sections are fun reading in and of themselves. **Dinosaurs** has an easy-to-read page of phonetic spellings.

These books are, as the series titles indicates, small enough to stick in a backpack pocket, but their quality and the amount of information in each is by no means undersized, rivaling that of much larger and more expensive books. Although the reading level is suitable for upper elementary, the information is detailed and specific enough for much older readers as well.—James Blasingame.

Bailey, Jacqui. **Sex, Puberty and All That Stuff: A Guide to Growing Up**. Barron's, 2004. 112p. $12.95 Trade pb. 978-0-7641-2992-6. PLB $21.99. 978-1-4352-6998-9. Glossary. Index. Illus. Further Reading.
VOYA February 2005. **5Q · 5P · M · J · S**

A large helping of straightforward, up-to-date information peppered with humor and bright, graphic illustrations make this book one of the best texts about sex for developing adolescents. Writing in a conversational voice that speaks directly to youth, Bailey explicitly addresses both the physiology and the psychology of puberty, while debunking the myths and answering questions about everything from pimples to pelvic exams. The first chapters deal with the biological realities of puberty, divided into "girl stuff" and "boy stuff." The text is splashed with colorful sidebars that define terminology and provide more in-depth information or practical advice about a wide range of topics. The middle of the book deals with relationships, starting with friendship and moving into romance, dating, and sex. Bailey stresses responsible decision making and explores why young people choose to have sex, tackling common myths and providing reasons not to have sex along with tips for saying no. The last third of the book, however, deals with the realities of sexual behavior, including pregnancy and sexually transmitted diseases, contraception, sexual abuse, and related legal issues.

The message Bailey reiterates is "Your body is your own . . . and no one has the right to make you do anything with it or to it that you don't want to do." To supplement her already brimming text, Bailey provides an annotated list of organizations and Web sites that provide additional information as well as a glossary of common terms. This book is one that many librarians and educators will wish that they had had when entering puberty.—Michele Winship.

Barnhouse, Rebecca. **The Book of the Maidservant**. Random House, 2009. 240p. $16.99. 978-0-375-85856-7. PLB $19.99. 978-0-375-95856-4. $6.99 pb. 978-0-375-85857-4.
   VOYA October 2009. **5Q · 5P · M · J · S**
      Young Johanna, living in fifteenth-century England, has been placed in the household of wealthy Dame Margery Kempe, an irritatingly devout woman given to loud displays of weeping for the sufferings of the Virgin Mary although she regularly abuses her servants. Dame Margery announces she will make a pilgrimage to Rome, and Johanna will accompany her as her personal maid. Johanna, who has never set foot outside her small town, prepares fearfully for a journey that quickly becomes one of drudgery and hardship. Dame Margery, greatly disliked by the other pilgrims, consigns Johanna to group servant and finally leaves them all, abandoning her. Evil pilgrim Petrus often beats Johanna and attempts to rape her in Venice, forcing Johanna to flee and use her wits to get to Rome. Despite betrayals, injuries, and near starvation, Johanna eventually finds sanctuary and a measure of peace in Rome's English hospice.
      This debut novel by a professor of medieval history is based upon the first autobiography in English, The Book of Margery Kempe. Johanna, who actually existed and is less attractively treated in that tome, becomes a real girl with her own point of view in this novel. Earthy, authentic, and engrossing, this fast-paced, easy read belongs on the shelf with Karen Cushman's **The Midwife's Apprentice** (Clarion, 1995/**VOYA** August 1995) and **Catherine, Called Birdie** (Clarion, 1994/**VOYA** June 1994).—Laura Woodruff.

Barry, Dave, and Ridley Pearson. **Peter and the Secret of Rundoon**. Hyperion/DBG, 2007. 463p. $18.99. 978-0-7868-3788-5. $8.99 pb. 978-1-4231-2326-2.
   VOYA February 2008. **5Q · 5P · M · J** (SF/F/H)
      The fate of all existence rests in the hands of Peter Pan and his allies in this gripping final installment of the *Starcatcher* series. After their previous adventures battling pirates and the shadowy malevolent beings known as "the Others," Peter, the orphaned "lost" boys, and Tinkerbell are trying to content themselves with a quiet life on Mollusk Island. When attacked by the savage Scorpion warriors, Peter and his friends escape only to be captured by the evil King Zarboff and brought to the exotic land of Rundoon. While imprisoned, Peter learns the dreadful Lord Ombra, the Others' leader, is still alive and implementing a diabolically dangerous plan to obtain more of the mysterious and powerful "starstuff." Peter also discovers shocking information about his parents and his true identity, and is forced to use his special abilities to help the Others. Meanwhile back in London, Molly, an aspiring member of the noble Starcatchers and Peter's would-be love interest, learns of the Others' threat. Molly and her friend George Darling head to Rundoon to help Peter and rescue Molly's father. Captain Hook and his band of pirates even play an unexpectedly heroic role as they get caught up in the action.

This thoroughly satisfying and fast-paced adventure blends humor and drama in a compelling and moving story about friendship and growing up. Although billed as the last book in the series, Barry and Pearson pose enough unresolved questions to create the possibility of further Peter Pan adventures.—Amy Luedtke.

Barry, Dave, and Ridley Peterson. **Peter and the Shadow Thieves**. Hyperion, 2006. 464p. $18.99. 978-0-7868-3787-8. $8.99 pb. 978-1-4231-2326-2.
VOYA August 2006. **5Q · 5P · M · J** (SF/F/H)

Peter Pan, Tinker Bell, and Captain Hook are back in this delightful sequel to the popular **Peter and the Starcatchers** (Hyperion, 2004/**VOYA** December 2004). The story begins with Peter and his fellow orphans living comfortably on the remote Mollusk Island, which they have dubbed Never Land. Molly, the intrepid heroine of the first book, is back in London with her parents, who are guardians of a powerful substance known as "starstuff." Peter's only problem is boredom, which he alleviates by taunting Captain Hook and the other marooned pirates. Peter also feels uneasy because the powers he has obtained from the starstuff, including the ability to fly and to never grow old, have forever set him apart from his friends. The peace of island life is shattered when the sinister Lord Ombra and his henchmen come searching for the starstuff. Ombra discovers the starstuff is in London with Molly's family, so Peter and Tink undertake a dangerous journey to warn Molly. Peter makes it to London in time to rescue Molly, but Molly's mother is kidnapped by Ombra.

This sequel is even better than its predecessor, with all the excitement and magic but more drama and suspense. Lord Ombra is a frightening and formidable villain, a not-quite-human creature who has the ability to control people by stealing their shadows. There is not quite as much humor here, but the more complex characters and relationships make the story more compelling. It is an exciting, rousing read perfect for fantasy adventure fans.—Amy Luedtke.

Baskin, Julia, et al. **The Notebook Girls**. Warner, 2006. 352p. $22.95. 978-0-446-57862-2. $22.95 Trade pb. 978-0-446-57862-2.
VOYA June 2006. **5Q · 5P · J · S · A/YA**
Popular Paperbacks for Young Adults 2007.

It is unusual to give a rave review to a book with no discernible plot and riddled with spelling and grammatical errors, but this one is a rather unusual book. When Sophie, Courtney, Julia, and Lindsey begin freshman year at New York City's prestigious Stuyvesant High School in 2001, they decide to create a shared diary to chronicle the ups and downs of their daily lives. Over several years, their notebook records gossip, dating, fighting, sex, experiments with drugs and alcohol, and their struggles with religion and sexuality. The notebook is presented as a facsimile of the original, containing the girls' own handwriting, photos, and doodling on each page. Their lives do not contain many of the dramatic issues often chronicled in young adult novels, such as pregnancy, violence, or addiction. Nevertheless it is a true and very humorous account of what is really happening in the lives of "good kids."

Teenage girls will love the realistic portrayal of the problems that they are facing, as well as the voyeuristic look into the lives of other girls. In no way does the book moralize or present dire consequences to the girls' actions, which might, along with some graphic language and artwork, trouble some parents. Both parents and educators of teenage girls, though, will want to read it to have a better understanding of what their girls are thinking and saying to one another privately. The notebook is highly recommended for all young adult collections.—Stephanie Petruso.

Bauer, Joan. **Stand Tall**. Putnam's, 2002. 192p. $16.99. 978-0-399-23473-6. $7.99 pb. 978-0-14-240427-0.
VOYA October 2002. **5Q · 5P · M · J**

As the tallest seventh grader in the history of his school, Tree has a lot to deal with both in and out of class. His parents' recent divorce forces him to alternate weeks between his strangely empty home with his father and grandfather and his mother's new apartment. Tree begins a friendship with an outcast eighth-grade girl and stands up against the meanness of some popular kids for the first time in his school career. He takes ballroom dancing classes with his losing basketball team, discusses the Vietnam War and war in general with his grandfather while helping him adjust to his prosthetic leg, cares for the old family dog, and helps clean up after his town is flooded. Through his relationships, he begins to take pride in himself and accept his height.

Bauer creates another book full of strong, memorable characters. Tree is a presence because of his size, and he is an intelligent, thoughtful character. His thoughts and feelings about the divorce are very real. Bauer explores his relationship with his brothers and the way that the divorce changes things. Tree's relationship with his grandfather is quite special, and through it, he learns how to find the good in anything that happens. Although the adults in the book make mistakes from time to time, Tree has an excellent relationship with each of them. This book will be enjoyed by all middle-school readers and will certainly satisfy Bauer fans.—Cindy Faughnan.

Berk, Josh. **The Dark Days of Hamburger Halpin**. Knopf/Random House, 2010. 256p. $16.99. 978-0-375-85699-0.
VOYA June 2010. **5Q · 5P · S**
Popular Paperbacks for Young Adults 2012.

Will Halpin takes a giant, uncertain leap when he leaves his school for the deaf to attend mainstream Carbon High School. He lands at the bottom of the social hierarchy, befriended by Devon Smiley, the kid who gets his swimming trunks flushed down the toilet by the popular football jocks. When one of these jocks is pushed into a coal shaft on a class field trip, Will and Devon team up for some serious, Hardy Boy-style detective work. Will's mad computer skills, his impressive ability to read lips, and his compelling need to uncover a truth buried in his own family tree, transform his awkward high school transition into a dangerous (but thrilling!) hunt for a killer.

Author Berk's first novel is a masterful combination of light humor and edgy suspense, moving seamlessly from playful mockery of the high school social scene to the very real destruction of lives. Will is a delightful narrator: smart, wry, and insightful. His experiences in the hearing world, as well as his reflections on deaf culture, add another level of interest in this already compulsively readable novel. Like Ted in **The London Eye Mystery** (Siobhan Dowd, 2008), who was able to solve a mystery because his brain ran on ". . . a different operating system," Will is empowered by the loss of one sense to develop skills that few hearing people can claim. Readers will get a fine life lesson: Never underestimate the hefty, deaf kid. This book would be an excellent selection for teen book clubs.—Diane Colson.

Bick, Ilsa. **Ashes**. Egmont, 2011. 480p. $17.99. 978-1-60684-175-4.
  VOYA October 2011. **5Q · 5P · M · J · S · A/YA**

Bick takes the best of post-apocalyptic, zombie fiction, like Cormac McCarthy's **The Road** (Vintage Books, 2007) and Robert Kirkman's *The Walking Dead* graphic novel series (Image Comics, 2006-2011), and adds the exact thing that has been sorely lacking from those genres: girl power, and in a heaping dose. Seeking reprieve from a terminal sentence, orphan Alex decides to spend her last days in the wilderness. When she meets a kindly old man and his snotty granddaughter, Ellie, Alex is eager to be alone, but noone is prepared for an electromagnetic pulse that leaves the old man dead and Alex with a recovered sense of smell and the new ability to discern fear. There are also a whole mess of ravenous adolescent cannibals, paranoid adults, and a ticked-off eight-year-old.

A child psychiatrist, aspiring surgeon, and former Air Force major, Bick has the background necessary to craft her tale, as her heroine faces situations that make the Hunger Games look like a tea party. Deceptively simple at first, the story is infused with science and real-life elements that lend further credence as the action picks up steam. Bick proves adept at tugging at heartstrings while gearing up for the next dreadful thing waiting around the corner. Oh sure, there are a few love interests in the mix, but don't mistake Alex for the shrinking-violet paranormal wisps or kick-rump world saviors flooding the YA market. She's better: A real girl with brains and heart, just trying to survive in a world that's out to eat her alive.—Matthew Weaver.

Bick, Ilsa J. **Draw the Dark**. Carolrhoda, 2010. 344p. $16.95. 978-0-7613-5686-8.
  VOYA December 2010. **5Q · 5P · S** (SF/F/H)

It is one thing to have your own bad memories—it is another to have the collective bad memories of a town filed away in your head. Christian knows this torment intimately, as he has taken to drawing the dark images that lace his mind. With both of his parents missing in action, he finds himself drawing inexplicable images and, worse yet, embattled in wars that he cannot recall creating. This loner discovers his sleepy town's nasty little secret of what really happened when the Nazis arrived. He also becomes a bit of an unsuspecting medium for connecting the town's past and present.

This offering is chock-full of action and vivid characterization. The plot is unique and highlights a time that is often overlooked in American history—it will keep readers engaged and wondering how it will all end. The author paints vivid depictions of Christian's mind, and the reader will be right there with him along for the ride. The ending will leave the reader holding on for dear life. The author has a few loose ends, but something this enthralling should never be expected to end neatly or conform to traditional literary notions. This title is a must for any school or public library—it is not to be missed.—Robbie L. Flowers.

Bitton-Jackson, Livia. **Hello, America: A Refugee's Journey from Auschwitz to the New World**. Simon Pulse, 2006, ©2005. 240p. $5.99 pb. 978-1-4169-1625-3.
VOYA April 2005. **5Q · 5P · M · J**

Continuing her memoir where **My Bridges of Hope** (Simon & Schuster, 1999/ **VOYA** June 1999) concluded with "to America and the hope of a better future," the third volume of Bitton-Jackson's personal story opens with the arrival of the SS General Stewart in the harbor of New York in 1951. Elli and her mother, Laura Friedmann, are fortunate enough to have survived Auschwitz and to have close family members already established in New York. Into the arms of brother and son, Bubi, and aunts and uncles willing to ease their transition, Elli's spirit is genuinely admired by good Dr. Alex, who becomes a confidante and then suitor. The reader is treated to Elli's refreshing perspective, from the first tastes of a milkshake and a tuna sandwich and adolescent experiences of sleepovers and first dates to inquisitive questions, such as "What is a department store?" and "What are bagels and lox?" Teens will easily identify with Elli's camp adventures, allowing her naïveté to underscore her lack of social development. When Elli becomes a teacher and is questioned by the children about the tattooed numbers on her arm, the poignant scene with her principal is shocking in its coldness.

This accurate, gentle narrative portrays an immigrant family with a profound understanding of the obstacles that had to be overcome to attain freedom and succeed at living the American dream. Each book reads independently, but the trilogy presents a significant addition to the memoirs of World War II and the Holocaust and is highly recommended for all middle school libraries.—Nancy Zachary.

Bogdan, D.L. **Rivals in the Tudor Court**. Kensington, 2011. 384p. $15. Trade pb. 978-0-7582-4200-6.
VOYA Online July 2011. **5P · 5Q · S**

In the time of Henry VIII of England, everyone was vying for the attention of the crown, if not for the crown itself. Thomas Howard was no different. Howard is obsessed with regaining power for the Howard family and will stop at nothing to gain it. Told in the first person from the perspectives of Thomas Howard, Elizabeth Howard, and Bess Holland, this gripping tale looks into the lives of the people in the thick of Henry's court, and takes you deep inside the minds of these major players to explore what truly motivated the deaths of several English queens.

The first person narrative gives the reader insight into a time very far removed from today's modern world. The mature content and language lends to the authenticity and reality of this tale. The reader is hearing the confessions of Thomas Howard as he tries to justify the motivations for his actions, and ultimately, his downfall. Even the deaths of his children and relatives do not deter his blind ambition. In contrast, Elizabeth Howard tells of her attempts to stay true to her queen even against her husband's wishes. Her plight tears at the heart and shows what true courage is: believing in things one knows are right even when others believe they are wrong. Last, but not least, Bess Holland tells of how she came to be in the middle of this husband and wife, and all the political maneuvers that Thomas Howard attempts to make. Neither woman is really in control of her situation, but both make due the best they can because nothing and no one can deter Thomas Howard.—Barbara Allen.

Bouchard, David and Pam Aleekuk. **Long Powwow Nights**. Illus. by Leonard Paul. Music by Buffy Sainte-Marie. Red Deer Press, 2009. 32p. $23.95. 978-0-88995-427-4.
VOYA June 2010. **5Q · 4P · M · J · S · A/YA**

This is a multisensory and multicultural gem. It utilizes poetry, music, and art to relate a story of powwow and intergenerational connection. The sub-title is Iskewsis . . . Dear Mother. The book is accompanied by a CD of song and music that the reader may listen to while following the text and viewing the full-page colored paintings. Either the book or the CD is complete individually, but they complement each other to increase the sensory experience of the reader. A reading/listening of this tale will stimulate imagination and reflection, as will the paintings depicting various participants in full attire. Teachers of all levels and disciplines will be able to utilize this resource as a springboard for a variety of creative activities for students. The text and songs are in English and in Mi'kmaq, a Canadian indigenous language.

The reader will be left with new insight into a traditional powwow with its mystic dancers and a daughter's remembrance of her mother through the ritual. The young at heart of all ages will relish this truly sensitive celebration of heritage and culture. This unique resource is a must for the library for youth.—Marilyn Brien.

Bowsher, Melodie. **My Lost and Found Life**. Bloomsbury, 2006. 350p. $16.95. 978-1-58234-736-3. $7.95 Trade pb. 978-1-59990-155-8.
VOYA October 2006. **5Q · 5P · M · J · S**

Self-absorbed, pampered, homecoming-queen-beautiful Ashley is days from graduating from Burlingame High and jetting to Hawaii with the senior class, when her bookkeeper mother vanishes and becomes wanted by police for embezzlement. Faced with mounting bills and imminent eviction from her lavish home, Bowsher's initially shallow character passes denial and struggles through multiple difficulties, growing from entitled suburban brat into a responsible, respectful, gainfully employed societal member. On her journey, Ashley ventures beyond her safety zone: partying with wild Tatiana, moving into a camper-trailer behind a gas station, watching her best friend Nicole leave for college, finding work in a funky city cyber café and coming to value its unique clientele, befriending a grandfather figure, finding-and-losing-love, and ultimately enrolling in college. Adults maintain significance throughout; including her mother's best friend and her mother's ex-boyfriend (both of whom initially view her as spoiled and demanding) Nicole's mother whose dislike is obvious, and the earnest Officer Strobel. Engrossed readers witness Ashley's amazing, wholly unexpected transformation with satisfaction and pride. What teens will read as a riveting adventure, adults might see as empowering teen readers. Ashley develops into a complex, admirable young woman.

Useful in classrooms as a vehicle for discussion of plot and character development, instrumental for engaging reluctant readers, and decidedly satisfying for all, this book belongs in schools and libraries where readers age twelve to twenty-seven can enjoy and learn from it.—Cynthia Winfield.

Boyce, Frank Cottrell. **Cosmic**. Walden Pond/HarperCollins, 2010. 313p. $16.99. 978-0-06-183683-1. PLB $17.89. 978-0-06-183686-2.
VOYA April 2010. **5Q · 5P · M**
Guardian Award — 2008 shortlist.
Carnegie Medal — 2009 shortlist.
Best Fiction for Young Adults 2011.

Liam, almost thirteen, is tall enough to be mistaken for a grown-up, especially when he sprouts facial hair. His ability to pass for much older leads to some hilarious episodes, some with his friend Florida who poses as his "princess" daughter. Their relationship—as they switch from friends to impersonating father and teenage daughter—is beautifully captured by Boyce. But when Liam receives a text message that he has been selected as a dad for the "Biggest Thrill Ride in the History of the World," he faces his biggest challenge yet. Taking Florida with him, he flies to China where he meets the other contestants—three ambitious fathers and their talented sons. Liam proves that he has the qualities to accompany the children on the "Rocket" into space despite being scorned by the other dads as "childish." He has, he is told, the right attitude because he is ready to learn.

Boyce brilliantly captures Liam's voice as he switches from a teen delighting, for example, in the sheer fun of being weightless (he feels like a "Power Ranger") to being the "Responsible Adult." Liam uses skills gained from playing Warcraft and Orbiter IV to guide the rocket back to earth when things go awry. His sense of awe and danger when he spacewalks and his crew's joyride to the moon on a solar-powered ship that looks like an "ice-cream van" are paralleled with fascinating facts about astronauts and the science of space travel. This superb humorous and inventive "cosmic" adventure celebrates space travel, friendships, and dads.—Hilary Crew."

Bray, Libba. **Rebel Angels**. *Gemma Doyle*. Delacorte, 2005. 560p. $16.95. 978-0-385-73029-7. $9.99 pb. 978-0-385-73341-0.
VOYA August 2005. **5Q · 5P · M · J · S** (SF/F/H)
Best Books for Young Adults 2006.
Teens Top Ten 2006.

Gemma Doyle, heroine of **A Great and Terrible Beauty** (Delacorte, 2004/**VOYA** April 2004), is not looking forward to Christmas. Other girls spend their holidays with family, sharing tender moments exchanging gifts, but Gemma must worry about keeping her father away from his laudanum bottle and enduring the company of her self-centered brother, Tom. Other girls dream of dancing sugar plums, but Gemma has nightmares of her dead friend, Pippa, holding a severed goat head and visions of a sinister girl trio who might-or might not-have accurate information about her nemesis, Circe. Coupled with these holiday woes, the Rakshana demands that she find an arcane temple in the otherworldly realms and bind the magic that she set loose when she smashed the runes at the conclusion of the earlier book. The only one who may know the temple's location is a Bedlam inmate who speaks in riddles.

This extraordinary novel moves along at breathtaking speed from beginning to end. Part history lesson, part gothic fantasy, part feminist manifesto, Bray's second book is astounding in scope. Although it is certainly imperative to read the first before plunging into its superior sequel, have no fear-those fuzzy on the events of the first novel need only read chapter four to catch up. Beloved characters Ann, Felicity, and Kartik return with both new and old personality quirks. Conspiracy theorists will be delighted with secret society intrigue propelled by the Rakshana, enigmatic Miss McCleethy, and ill-fated Nell Hawkins. Librarians should have little difficulty booktalking this excellent addition to their collection.—Angelica Delgado.

Brennan, Herbie. **The Secret Prophecy**. Balzer + Bray/HarperCollins, 2012. 368p. $16.99. 978-0-06-207180-4.

VOYA August 2012. **5Q · 5P · M · J · S**

When Em's father dies suddenly and his mother is locked up in a psychiatric hospital, Em begins to suspect his father's death was actually murder. As Em investigates what his professor father was working on up until his death, he begins to uncover a trail of lies he never knew existed.

Brennan has written a masterpiece thriller of intrigue, suspense, and mystery—a well written novel that readers will not want to put down. Any person who enjoys getting lost within the pages of a book will want to pick up this one. With sharp characters and appropriate language, Brennan's title is for people age ten to adult. It is a must-read that readers will want to share with others.—Juli Henley.

Brown, Jennifer. **Hate List**. Little, Brown, 2009. 416p. $16.99. 978-0-316-04144-7. $8.99 Trade pb. 978-0-316-04145-4.

VOYA December 2009. **5Q · 5P · S**

Popular Paperbacks for Young Adults 2012.

Best Books for Young Adults 2010.

Valerie returns to school after her boyfriend, Nick, opened fire on many of their classmates and a teacher before killing himself. It is a tough scenario for anyone to face, but the survivors view her with hatred and suspicion. In selecting his victims, Nick used the list they made in what she thought was a means of blowing off steam. It contained all the people who treated them badly. Valerie must contend with the gossip and glares at school and at home, as her parents freak at the slightest hint of adolescent angst. In addition, Valerie must reconcile the image of Nick as a monster with the tender, troubled, Shakespeare-loving boy who also loved her. How can she mourn him while dealing with what he did?

This novel ought to be the last written about a fictional high school shooting because it is difficult to imagine any capable of handling it better. Brown deftly traverses highly controversial ground with a respectful touch that never veers into sensationalism. She never bends to stereotypes nor settles for easy answers. The finale is a pitch-perfect tribute to the people who died or bear scars from Nick's actions, but there is no satisfying conclusion, which is itself satisfying. Also noteworthy: for a therapist, Brown gives Valerie Dr. Rex Hieler, easily one of the best adult characters in YA literature. He provides an oasis of comfort for both the character and readers in a story that is as sensitive and honest as it is spellbinding.—Matthew Weaver.

Bujold, Lois McMaster. **The Curse of Chalion**. EOS/HarperCollins, 2001. 442p. $13.95 Trade pb. 978-0-06-113424-1. $7.99 pb. 978-0-380-81860-0.
VOYA December 2001. **5Q · 5P · S · A/YA** (SF/F/H)
Mythopoeic Fantasy Award for Adult Literature 2002.

As a former courtier and soldier, the man on the road to Valenda is almost unrecognizable. Broken and scarred, Cazaril has survived the torturous life of a slave in the enemy galleys only to find himself without a home and with only the hope that someone might recognize him and give him shelter in the castle where he once worked as a page. He is taken in and given a job, not in the kitchen or the stables as he had hoped but rather as the personal secretary of the Royesse Iselle, the sister of the next ruler of the land. His hopes of quietly living out the rest of his days are dashed when he becomes inextricably involved in the political intrigue and magical curses that surround the royal family. Cazaril finds himself drawn between the will of the gods and the wills of the men around him as he struggles to assure that the throne will go to a just heir and that the crown will not be thrown to the very men who schemed to enslave him many years before.

Subtle yet powerful language raises this fantasy above most others in its genre, making it impossible to put down. The interplay of will and destiny creates a thoughtful novel, while the crashing swords and the dark magical powers make it an exciting read. With its challenging vocabulary and artful writing style, Bujold's latest novel might just be what older Harry Potter fans are yearning for.—Heather Hepler.

Burns, Loree Griffin. **Tracking Trash: Flotsam, Jetsam, and the Science of Ocean Motion**. *Scientists in the Field*. Houghton Mifflin, 2007. 64p. $18. 978-0-618-58131-3. $8.99 Trade pb. 978-0-547-32860-7. Glossary. Index. Illus. Photos. Maps. Charts. Biblio. Further Reading.
VOYA February 2007. **5Q · 5P · M · J · S**

On May 27, 1990, a cargo ship carrying goods from Korea to the United States in the Pacific Ocean dumped twenty-one of its cargo containers into the sea during a storm. Five of those containers were packed with Nike sneakers. Within months, these sneakers began showing up on beaches in and around Seattle, drawing the attention of Curt Ebbesmeyer, a scientist who studies ocean currents. For three years, Ebbesmeyer collected data on the sneakers washing up on shore and realized that they represented the largest oceanographic drift experiment ever undertaken. This book explains the science of studying ocean motion through tracking plastic trash that has made it into the sea through cargo spills or storm drains. The text is packed with full-color photos of the scientists at work as well as some pretty disturbing facts. Between mainland United States and the Hawaiian islands, there is a floating plastic garbage dump as big as the state of Alaska. There are also huge masses of discarded fishing nets-ghost nets-entangling all forms of sea life and drifting into coral reefs, creating massive destruction.

The writing is light, but the facts are weighty, and the message of reduce, reuse, and recycle comes across loud and clear. This book is fascinating on its own, but it also can hold its place in a middle-level science curriculum. The complex science behind the movement of the ocean is explained clearly with excellent supporting graphics. Additional books and Web sites are included for further study.—Michele Winship.

Card, Orson Scott. **Ender in Exile**. *Ender*. Tor, 2008. 373p. $25.95. 978-0-7653-0496-4. $7.99 pb. 978-0-7653-4415-1.
VOYA December 2008. **5Q · 5P · M · J · S** (SF/F/H)

Margaret Edwards Award-winner Card's latest entry in the *Ender* series goes back to the first book, **Ender's Game** (Tor, 1985). In fact, this novel essentially takes the last chapter of **Ender's Game** and expands it to novel length. Ender is thirteen, the hero of the world for destroying the formics. But where does a thirteen-year-old hero live? Ender and his sister Valentine, who has just retired as the demagogue Demosthenes, go to a colony planet where Ender will become the governor. Ender is obsessed with the formics, particularly with wondering why the hive queens allowed him to destroy their planet. At the same time, he must deal with human concerns, such as the power-hungry captain of the ship that is taking him to the colony world and the Italian girl and her mother who see Ender as a "young man with prospects."

Card does not disappoint as he explores ideas and human nature through Ender's eyes. Much of the novel consists of dialogue and e-mails, and these devices keep the book moving along at a rapid clip. Even though readers of **Ender's Game** and its other sequels and companion books will not be in doubt as to the resolution of this book, Card keeps the tension going. Fans, especially those who enjoyed the first *Ender* book and the *Shadow* companion books, will be delighted to learn more about the teenaged Ender and his journeys.—Sarah Flowers.

_____. **First Meetings in the Enderverse**. Tor, 2003. 224p. $6.99 pb. 978-0-7653-4798-5.
VOYA February 2004. **5Q · 5P · J · S · A/YA** (SF/F/H)

Orson Scott Card not only reissues his classic novella *Ender's Game*--first published in **Analog** magazine in 1977 and then later expanded to a full novel in 1985 (Tor)—but also offers two prequels and a sequel in **First Meetings in the Enderverse**. Suitably sardonic illustrations by Craig Phillips add to the pleasure of revisiting the Wiggin clan. In *The Polish Boy*, an agent of the Hegemony, recruiting military talent to aid in the war against the Buggers, discovers John Paul Wiggin. This precocious future father of Andrew "Ender" Wiggin, buried in a Polish Catholic family whose resistance to the authorities earned only poverty, bargains for an education in the U.S. and concomitant freedom for his family. But he must pay a price in the future, as in the folktale Rumpelstiltskin. In *Teacher's Pet*, written especially for this collection, john Paul Wiggin has developed into an obnoxiously arrogant graduate student at an American university. With stubborn persistence, he proclaims his intention to marry his brilliant professor, Theresa Brown, and finally wears down her scornful resistance. Then there is the famous story, *Ender's Game*, in which the relentlessly competitive Wiggin undergoes layer after layer of training until, at the still tender age of twelve, he defeats the enemy Buggers. His strategies are stunningly clever, the discipline he asserts over himself and his soldiers is cruelly exhausting, and the final betrayal of this child leader is heartrending. It is a story to savor over and over. The final offering, *The investment Counselor*, takes place many years after Ender's conquest of the Buggers. Now a fabulous wealthy twenty- year-old, Ender travels incognito with his sister, Valentine, because the fickle general public considers him a despicable traitor. When his identity is almost revealed by a tax inspector, his privacy and his fortune are saved by a most unlikely source.

The added novellas work well together, maintaining Card's careful balance between cynicism and respect for human decency but at a more superficial and lighter level that gives relief to the power of the original tale. His easily readable style, fast-paced action, and perceptively drawn characters appeal to most readers, even those who claim to dislike science fiction.—Suzanne Reid.

_____. **Shadow of the Hegemon**. *Ender*. Tor, 2000. 363p. $25.95. 978-0-312-87651-7. $7.99 pb. 978-0-8125-6595-9.
VOYA June 2001. **5Q · 5P · J · S · A/YA** (SF/F/H)
Best Books for Young Adults 2002.

This sequel to **Ender's Shadow** (Tor, 1999/**VOYA** *Voyages*, February 2000) continues the story from Bean's viewpoint and takes place in roughly the same time period as the beginning of **Speaker for the Dead** (Tor, 1986/**VOYA** August/October 1986). Ender has left the planet, but Bean and the other members of Ender's Dragon Army are suddenly the targets of kidnappers. Bean barely escapes being blown up-twice-but Petra Arkanian, another of Ender's "jeesh," is not so lucky. She is captured by the psychopathic Achilles, Bean's enemy from his days in the streets of Rotterdam. Achilles is using Petra and other Battle School alumni to help him determine how to take over the world militarily. Meanwhile, Locke, also known as Peter Wiggin, Ender's brother, is working on his own plan to control the world by more peaceful means and become Hegemon, with Bean as his shadow, or background aide.

As always with Card, brilliant young people face deadly peril, participate in fast-paced action and heroic deeds, and deal with genuine moral dilemmas with intelligence and thoughtfulness. Some issues are left unresolved, paving the way for another sequel, which no doubt will be welcomed warmly by the many fans of Card and of this series.—Sarah Flowers.

Cart, Michael et al. **911: The Book of Help**. Cricket Books, 2002. 192p. $17.95. 978-0-8126-2659-9. $9.95 Trade pb. 978-0-8126-2676-6.

VOYA October 2002. **5Q · 5P · M · J · S** (NF)

As the nation honors the anniversary of that terrible September morning, one of what surely will be many books about the tragedy offers readers a chance to plumb the depths of their thoughts and feelings. This remarkable collection of authors writing in response to the tragic events of 9/11 is divided into four sections. In the first section, Healing, the entries range from factual accounts of working at Ground Zero by David Paterson to Sonya Sones' evocative poem "Voices." Noted authors Jim Murphy, Susan Cooper, And Avi join others in a second section labeled Searching for History, an attempt to place the events into a historical and yet personal context. Asking Why? Why? Why? features works by Virginia Euwer Wolff, Suzanne Fisher Staples, Marc Aronson, Marina Budhos, and Nikki Giovanni, each struggling to understand the events. Readers discover that there might not be many answers. Finally, a section called Reacting and Recovering offers poems and essays from Arnold Adoff, Sharon Creech, and Naomi Shihab Nye among other luminaries of the juvenile book industry.

This collection is not an easy book. Many readers will find themselves welling with tears as they read these intensely personal pieces. Nevertheless there might just be some healing in the examination of the scars left from that day. Recommend this book to English teachers in search of memoirs to share with students, to history teachers looking for some way to begin discussions about social issues, and to teens wanting to scrutinize their reactions in light of others' responses. In short, here is a book too good not to share with all readers.—Teri Lesesne.

Cart, Michael, Ed. **Love and Sex: Ten Stories of Truth for Teens**. Simon Pulse, 2003, ©2001. $13.95 Trade pb. 978-0-689-85668-6.

VOYA June 2001. **5Q · 5P · S**

Best Books for Young Adults 2002.

The cool purple-and-silver cover that features shadowed teens at a rave, and the provocative title of Cart's newest compilation will ensure its circulation at libraries anywhere. It is an added bonus that the subtle, finely tuned stories inside are just as high caliber as the packaging promises. The stories are arranged in the order that love and sex develop for teens, from fumbling first times all the way through to coming to terms with one's sexual identity. Joan Bauer's *Extra Virgin* starts by describing how abstaining is an easier talk than walk when you finally meet that perfect someone. Laurie Halse Anderson puts a postmodern spin on the story of Adam and Eve in *Snake*, and Chris Lynch humorously tackles the constantly changing nature of adolescent desire in *The Cure for Curtis*. In *The Acuteness of Desire*, Michael Lowenthal sensitively explores the pain and confusion that ensues when a young man reveals his crush on a male classmate. In *Troll Bumps*, Shelley Stoehr's ardent teen heroine is surprised to discover that sometimes infatuation just . . . ends. The best story in the bunch just might be *The Welcome*, Emma Donoghue's amazing narrative about a young lesbian who lives in a group home and learns that the housemate she has a crush on is really a young man working through transgender issues.

Cart's compilation is nothing short of luminous, each story shedding light on a different sexual topic with which teens struggle. This collection is highly recommended for high school fans of E. R. Frank's **Life Is Funny** (DK, 2000/**VOYA** June 2000) and Gary Paulsen's **Beet Fields** (Random House, 2000/**VOYA** December 2000).—Jennifer Hubert.

Carter, Ally. **Out of Sight, Out of Time: Gallagher Girls**. Hyperion, 2012. 304p. $16.99. 978-1-4231-4794-7.
VOYA June 2012. **5Q · 5P · M · J · S**

The last thing Cammie can remember is leaving school grounds before the end-of-year finals, so how did she wind up in the Swiss Alps over three months later, surrounded by an unfamiliar gathering of Sisters. After her rapid extraction by Headmistress Morgan of the Gallagher Academy for Exceptional Young Women, aka Cammie's mom, it becomes obvious nothing is the same and everything is different. Zach and Dr. Steve have been accepted into the Academy, Aunt Abby is the new Covert-Ops instructor, and Cammie's friends do not seem to like her much anymore. So, what is a spy-girl to do but try and put the pieces of the puzzle together? Where did she go over those summer months; how did the Circle capture her; and who can she turn to in trust now that she is not sure she can trust in herself?

This reader consumed the entire book in one sitting, despite the fact that there will be a long wait until the next title in the series arrives. In defense, there was no way to stop turning the pages. How could one more chapter not be read when they kept ending in such a mysterious manner? This episode is nearly three hundred pages of perfection, and the only regret fans will have when they are done is being one step closer to the final installment of this outstanding series. At this point, the cliffhanger question becomes: is the reader's mental constitution tough enough to stand the suspense?—Stacey Hayman.

Cashore, Kristin. **Bitterblue**. Dial/Penguin, 2012. 576p. $19.99. 978-0-8037-3473-9.
VOYA June 2012. **5Q · 5P · J · S**
YALSA Readers' Choice List 2013

It has been eight years since Katsa and Po, heroes of **Graceling** (Penguin, 2008/**VOYA** October 2008), rescued ten-year-old Bitterblue from her evil father, King Leck, and helped her assume the throne of Monsea. Leck had the Grace, or special gift, of clouding people's minds so that they would accept whatever he told them. Horrible atrocities were committed in his name, leaving the kingdom deeply scarred. Queen Bitterblue suspects her advisors are not telling her the truth about conditions in her kingdom, distracting her instead with piles of paperwork. Frustrated by their obfuscation, she sneaks out at night to investigate for herself. Through new acquaintances Saf and Toby, she learns of an underground society of "truthseekers" who try to illuminate the past so that Monsea can finally heal. Now someone is targeting the truthseekers, and Bitterblue finds that even queens are not immune from danger. Who can she trust, in palace or city?

Fans of Cashore's **Graceling** and its companion **Fire** (Penguin, 2009/**VOYA** October 2009) will welcome this third (and final?) volume. Bitterblue struggles to grow into her role as ruler. She must learn not only the mechanics of governing but also the grace-with-a-small-g of mercy and forgiveness. The lengthy story is complicated, but readers will gallop through it, eager to catch up on beloved characters and hopeful that the Seven Kingdoms can at last find peace. There are astonishing and sometimes heartbreaking discoveries to be made before that can occur. Buy all three volumes, in multiple copies. As in Cashore's other stories, there are a few tasteful sex scenes.—Kathleen Beck.

Chappell, Crissa-Jean. **Total Constant Order**. Katherine Tegen Books, 2007. 288p. $16.99. 978-0-06-088605-9. PLB $17.89. 978-0-06-088606-6.
VOYA April 2008. **5Q · 5P · S**

Fin craves the solace of numbers and ritual. Numbers are constantly pounding out rhythms in her head, her only safety net in a world marred by high school cliques and the end of her parents' marriage. And that is before Fin finds the medication that is supposed to offer her a break from the prison of her obsessive compulsive mind. But another form of salvation comes to her through a mysterious graffiti artist. How does he speak to her and understand the rhythms of her mind? Could it be that there is someone out there who suffers like she does? When she meets Thayer, she discovers that she is not alone. Thayer is someone who can understand her therapy visits and the ups and downs of being medicated. The question becomes, how will Fin find herself in a fog of Paxil, angst, and confusion?

This must-have story is fresh. Chappell's first novel is a breakthrough. She manages to bring the audience into the mind of a teen suffering from OCD (obsessive compulsive disorder). Fin is a gritty character whose raw emotions speak to the reader. The author immerses her readers into Fin's mind and does not relent on the book's edgy voice.—Robbie L. Flowers.

Chima, Cinda Williams. **The Demon King**. *A Seven Realms Novel*. Hyperion/DBG, 2009. 512p. $17.99. 978-1-4231-1823-7. $9.99 pb. 978-1-4231-2136-7.
VOYA October 2009. **5Q · 5P · M · J · S** (SF/F/H)
Best Fiction for Young Adults 2011.
Popular Paperbacks for Young Adults 2012.

The mountain city of Fellsmarch is home to both Han "Cuffs" Alister and Raisa ana'Helena, but they might as well be worlds apart. Han has set aside his life of crime as the head of the Raggers street gang for the sake of his younger sister, Mari, and seeks to bring in through honest means enough to feed Mari and his mother. His best friend, Fire Dancer, lives outside town at the Marisa Pines Camp, and the two young men often hunt together. One afternoon, their mountainside hunting excursion nearly turns deadly when they encounter three young wizards causing trouble. Through wit and bravado, they escape with Han in possession of a very powerful amulet. Raisa, the princess heir of the Fells, observes things changing too quickly for her taste. Her mother, the queen, falls under the dangerous influence of the High Wizard, and civil war erupts in the surrounding countryside. Her childhood friend, Amon Byrne, returns from three years of training taller, more handsome, and a member of the Queen's Guard. Raisa's important

Name Day (sixteenth birthday) quickly approaches, when she will be formally eligible for marriage.

Not surprisingly to those familiar with the earlier *Heir Trilogy*, Chima succeeds beautifully again in creating a fully orbed world. Her characters have depth and richness, and the two main characters (whose stories are told in alternating chapters) provide emotional vestment for readers of both genders. Themes of political and magical power, love, sacrifice, courage, and even revisionist history recur throughout the tale and offer the intelligent reader food for thought. The pacing of the narrative and revelation of secrets make the execution of the story itself breathtaking and an excellent choice for reluctant readers. A virtually flawless tale, this book will leave readers anxiously awaiting the next novel in *The Seven Realms*.—Melissa Moore.

_____. **The Dragon Heir**. *The Heir Trilogy*. Hyperion/DBG, 2008. 512p. $17.99. 978-1-4231-1070-5. $8.99 Trade pb. 978-1-4231-1071-2.
VOYA October 2008. **5Q · 5P · M · J** (SF/F/H)
USA Today bestseller

Jason Haley has to find a way to make a difference. Discovering the dragon's hoard might be the ticket, but Leander Hastings makes Jason take the amulets, sword, and most important, the Dragonheart, to Trinity, Ohio, for safe keeping. Ever since Madison Moss took the hit of dark magic intended for Seph McCauley, she has had terrifying nightmares, and her touch makes Seph ill. Warren Barber, Claude and Devereaux D'Orsay, and the heads of the White and Red Roses seek to control the Dragonheart stone, the source of power for the magical guilds. As unlikely alliances form and Weir converge on Trinity, the stage is set for the final battle.

The thrilling *Heir Trilogy* concludes with this beautifully directed tale of color and character, smells and spells. The backstory of the Dragonheart and the creation of the guilds are complex. Characters are developed in depth rather than breadth, giving the tale an even greater richness than the first two novels. Some characters surprise with their actions-or lack thereof-giving the tale an unpredictability often not found in fantasy. With almost each chapter comes a change in focus, and yet each thread pulls together from across the globe to center in Trinity, creating a Weirweb destined to draw in readers.—Melissa Moore.

_____. **The Exiled Queen**. *A Seven Realms Novel*. Hyperion, 2010. 586p. $17.99. 978-1-4231-1824-4.
VOYA October 2010. **5Q · 5P · M · J · S** (SF/F/H)

Princess Raisa has fled from a forced marriage with Micah Bayar and traveled with Amon Byrne to Oden's Ford, where she hopes to pass as a normal soldier and get some valuable military training. Han Alister, still grieving the loss of his mother and sister, has also come to Oden's Ford, and with the companionship of Dancer and Cat, he hopes to develop his newly discovered wizarding abilities. Han proves to be a powerful wizard sought by others—Micah, the mysterious Crow, even Dean Abelard—but whom can he trust? And Raisa (known as Rebecca at the school) is drawn to both Amon and Han, yet both are forbidden to her.

Vividly drawn and lusciously executed, the *Seven Realms* series continues to grow in breadth and detail with this sequel to **The Demon King** (Hyperion, 2009/**VOYA** October 2009). The story lines are intricately plotted and the characters fully realized, even as questions about truth, loyalty, and power are explored. The pacing of the story is pitch-perfect, with the focus shifting back and forth from Han to Raisa until their paths merge, making this an excellent choice for reluctant readers who refuse to be put off by the size of the book. Readers may be reminded of Hogwarts (with the beautifully imagined Oden's Ford) or the *Twilight* (Little Brown Young Readers) books (with the passionate and forbidden feelings Raisa experiences), yet the novel stands on its own and will leave readers once again begging for more.—Melissa Moore.

_____. **The Warrior Heir**. *The Heir Trilogy*. Hyperion, 2007, ©2006. 448p. $8.99 pb. 978-0-7868-3917-9.
VOYA February 2006. **5Q · 5P · M · J · S** (SF/F/H)
Popular Paperbacks for Young Adults 2008.

Jack is a typical sixteen-year-old-good friend, average soccer player, living in Ohio with his mom who works too much. When he skips his medicine one day, the unthinkable happens: Jack is much stronger and faster and feels as if he is truly alive. Only now there are wizards coming out of the woodwork, seeking alternately to woo and kill Jack. Because of the stone implanted in his chest during infancy, Jack is a warrior expected to duel to the death on behalf of one of the wizarding houses. Quicker than he would like, training begins for the most momentous event in his young life, and Jack must decide whom he will serve and how he will survive.

Twists and turns abound in this remarkable, nearly flawless debut novel that mixes a young man's coming-of-age with fantasy and adventure. Fast paced and brilliantly plotted, Jack's journey is physical, mental, and emotional as he discovers his own identity and makes tough choices that impact others. Original, well-drawn characters are frequently revealed to be more than they appear, and Chima's writing richly portrays the mounting tension as Jack's options are methodically taken away. Readers of all ages will find in Jack a hero, who seeks above all to make the right choices regardless of the cost to himself (reminiscent of Harry Potter and Frodo Baggins). The resolution is clean but not idealized and fortunately leaves the door open for a sequel.—Melissa Moore.

_____. **The Wizard Heir**. *The Heir Trilogy*. Hyperion, 2008, ©2007. 480p. $8.99 Trade pb. 978-1-4231-0488-9.
VOYA June 2007. **5Q · 5P · M · J · S** (SF/F/H)

Seph McCauley knows that he is different. The magical powers that flow from his fingertips keep causing trouble and have now landed him at the Havens, a secluded private school in Maine. Seph needs wizard training, but when headmaster Gregory Leicester reveals that he also is a wizard and can train Seph to control his powers, the cost is too steep. When all hope seems lost, Linda Downey appears seemingly out of nowhere to spirit Seph away and give him the help he needs. Leicester does not give up, though, and will use whatever means necessary to gain control of Seph and his extraordinary power.

Fans of **The Warrior Heir** (Hyperion/DBG, 2006/**VOYA** February 2006) will be thrilled with this exceptional follow-up novel. The two wizarding houses are still at odds with each other, determining what the future will look like, and the other Weir classes (seers, enchanters, and warriors) are seeking refuge in the Sanctuary. Jack Swift and Ellen Stephenson, Leander Hastings, and of course, Downey are joined by richly drawn characters such as Seph and Leicester. This story is tighter, more complex, and even more intense than the first novel, moving the narrative forward at a determined pace. The atmosphere is brooding and heavy, sometimes almost oppressive. Chima uses her pen like a wand and crafts a wonderfully rich web of magic, while thankfully leaving some dangling threads for subsequent tales.—Melissa Moore.

Clare, Cassandra. **City of Lost Souls: The Mortal Instruments, Book 5**. McElderry/Simon & Schuster, 2012. 538p. $19.99. 978-1-4442-1686-4.
VOYA August 2012. **5Q · 5P · J · S** (SF/F/H)

It has been two weeks since Jace and Sebastian disappeared off the rooftop, leaving no traceable clues behind. Clary, the Lightwoods, Magnus, Simon, and the Clave are all on the hunt, hoping to save Jace and end the threat of Sebastian. Learning that the two are irrevocably bonded—harm one and they both bleed, kill one and they both die—and witnessing Jace's willing acceptance of Sebastian's directives are not enough to dissuade Clary from taking the risky, or foolish, opportunity to go on the run with Jace. Can Clary discover Sebastian's dark plan and reveal it to "Team Good" in time? Can Jace be saved from Sebastian's destruction, or even from himself, in the end?

As the relationships of the main and secondary characters continue to develop through this fifth book in the contemporary series, there is a greater focus on the somewhat bumpy progression of previously established couples and the introduction of newly defined pairings. There are particularly sweet moments shared between Magnus and Alec and Simon and Isabelle, as the two couples receive well-deserved time in the spotlight. It can be inferred that two of these couples are having sex, but nothing is addressed directly. Some readers might be unsettled by Sebastian's romantic interest in his sister, but his lack of recognizable human emotions makes this both more and less understandable. More of the Shadowhunter mythology, as well as the Downworlder society, is explained, giving longtime fans new details to ponder and dissect during lengthy discussions of what might lie ahead in book six, **City of Heavenly Fire**. If a cliff-hanger can be considered satisfying, then this book delivers.—Stacey Hayman.

_____. **Clockwork Angel**. *The Infernal Devices*. McElderry Books/Simon & Schuster, 2010. 496p. $19.99. 978-1-4169-7586-1.
VOYA October 2010. **5Q · 5P · J · S** (SF/F/H)
Teens' Top Ten 2011.

Tessa, a sixteen-year-old orphan, travels solo across the Atlantic to Victorian England to join her brother in London. But her brother doesn't meet her at the port—the Dark Sisters do. The Sisters keep Tessa captive while teaching her to use her "talent," the ability to change into anyone else, dead or alive. Eventually Tessa is rescued and thrust into a fight between the Shadowhunters and the Downworlders. In a world of new friends and enemies, vampires, werewolves, and automatons, Tessa isn't sure who to trust. But she must act to ensure the victory of the demon hunters and save her brother.

Sold as a prequel to the *Mortal Instrument* (McElderry Books/Simon & Schuster) series, this highly anticipated novel is the first of an expected trilogy. The *Mortal Instruments* series started with **City of Bones** (2007), continued with **City of Ashes** (2008) and **City of Glass** (2009), and a fourth book, **City of Fallen Angels**, will be published in March 2011. Steampunk is hot, and Clare conquered it! Methodically researched, her Victorian London is dark and romantic, and the strong-willed Tessa is an unexpected hero readers will love. Her love interest, Will, is the bad boy only Tessa can understand, while the sweet James is a possibility, too. At completion, the reader has more questions than answers, but the clarity of writing and quick plot turns will ensure its popularity.—Sarah Hill.

_____. **Clockwork Prince: The Infernal Devices, Book Two**. Margaret K. McElderry/Simon & Schuster, 2011. 528p. $19.99. 978-1-4169-7588-5.
VOYA December 2011. **5Q · 5P · J · S** (SF/F/H)
YALSA Reader's Choice List 1013

Many times second books in a series fall short of readers' expectations. Not so with **Clockwork Prince**. From the first page, readers are in the grip of an almost Shakespearean rollercoaster ride with a curse, a betrayal, a death, a secret marriage, a proposal, an impending birth, a long-lost relative, magic, and love—both given and unrequited—and behind the scenes are the Magister and all his clockwork machines and machinations. All the main characters from the first book are back, and there is the addition of the Lightwoods and Consul Weyland, as well as items such as the Mortal Sword and Book of the White. Tessa is still attracted to both Will and Jem but is more concerned with finding out who—and, perhaps, what—she is since the clues only manage to deepen the mystery. Will and Jem become more human and less warriors, with Jem teaching Tessa more about the Clave and Shadowhunters and Will's desire to drive everyone away finally explained. All the other characters also become more complete. Story lines begun in the first book are continued, with few resolved, but most new twists are completed.

Clare's books never disappoint, and this one will have readers clamoring for its sequel. Have more than one copy to meet the demand, but suggest that **Clockwork Angel** (Simon & Schuster, 2010/**VOYA** October 2010) be read first because this is not a sequel that can stand alone.—Suanne Roush.

Clement-Moore, Rosemary. **Hell Week**. *Maggie Quinn: Girl vs. Evil*. Delacorte, 2008. 368p. $16.99. 978-0-385-73414-1. PLB $19.99. 978-0-385-90429-2. $9.99 Trade pb. 978-0-385-73415-8.
VOYA August 2008. **5Q · 5P · S** (SF/F/H)

Maggie is starting her freshman year of college at Bedivere University. The downside is living at home. The upside would be turning her summer internship at the local paper into an ongoing job, in addition to seeing more of potential boyfriend Justin, a graduate student at the same school. When Maggie decides to join Sorority Rush for an investigative article, she has no idea that she has opened a Pandora's Box of trouble. The local paper passes, but the college paper wants Maggie to become the Phantom Pledge and write about her experiences. She chooses Sigma Alpha Xi. Maggie's gut feeling is that something strange is going on in the SAXi house and the SAXi sisters seem to know about her psychic abilities that readers learned about in **Prom Dates from Hell** (Delacorte, 2007). As the pledge process progresses, Maggie's lucky breaks increase and her intuitive insights decrease. What is really going on in the SAXi house, bringing unbelievable good fortune to its pledges, members, and alumni?

This reader has found a new series to love. The first book was a great start, and this installment is top-notch fun and a satisfying follow-up for older teens. Great dialogue and smart, interesting relationships that grow and change make both books a joy to read. There is endless potential in these characters and in their lives. Be aware Maggie is in college and acts true to her age. Also the demons Maggie faces are succubi, stealing their power through sex. Underage drinking is briefly talked about, but Maggie does not partake.—Stacy Hayman.

Clement-Moore, Rosemary. **Highway to Hell.** *Maggie Quinn: Girl vs. Evil.* Delacorte, 2009. 368p. PLB $19.99. 978-0-385-90462-9. $9.99 Trade pb. 978-0-385-73464-6.
VOYA February 2009. **5Q · 5P · S** (SF/F/H)
Best Books for Young Adults 2010.

The mysterious forces of Good and Evil come together for another throwdown and it's a lucky thing that Maggie is leading Team Good. The college freshman and her best friend, Lisa, are working on a new rite of passage into adulthood with a road trip to a beach for spring break. On the way to South Padre Island, the girls hit literal and metaphysical obstacles that prevent them from leaving Dulcina, a little town in the middle of nowhere Texas. Something is killing the livestock. A small faction says coyote have been driven to kill bigger prey than usual, but a more vocal group is naming it el chupacabra. Lisa's potential crush, Zeke Velasquez, might belong to the most powerful family of Velasquez County, but his refusal to consider a supernatural predator may be endangering everyone. Soon Justin arrives bringing his best friend and future priest, Henry, to even the odds of survival for the side of Good. Using local mojo, religious faith, and Maggie's gifts, the Evil One should be headed down for the count.

As Maggie's abilities develop, the opposing forces also seem to be getting stronger. It is great to witness her confidence grow, sending a subtle message to the reader about the strength of believing in oneself. Although there is more action, adventure, and suspense than in the two previous books about Maggie Quinn, the friendships and budding romances remain equally important. It is difficult to imagine teens who have enjoyed *Charmed*, *Buffy*, or the *Twilight* books not loving this series.—Stacey Hayman.

Cohn, Rachel. **You Know Where to Find Me.** Simon & Schuster, 2008. 208p. $16.99. 978-0-689-87859-6. $17.99 PLB. 978-1-4395-9485-8. $8.99 Trade pb. 978-0-689-87860-2.
VOYA February 2009. **5Q · 5P · S**

Cousins Miles and Laura grow up more like sisters, only months apart in age, sharing dreams and escapes. They were so tightly bonded that when Laura kills herself, an abandoned Miles barely functions. Laura was everything Miles wished for—beautiful, thin, and popular with boys. Miles loved her most, and living without her is a sentence in itself. During the summer after Laura's death, Miles, addicted to escapes—whether books, food, pills, or fantasies—does not realize how much she contributes to the lives of others.

Exquisitely written and delicately told, this story belongs to Miles. Cohn wisely focuses on her and gives the reader just enough of Laura to validate Miles's grief. But Miles does not stand in isolation; the book includes a rich circle of people very involved in the world and willing to anchor Miles in that world despite her courageous stubbornness. The completeness of the book is impressive. It is an intense and fulfilling read by a skillful storyteller.—C. J. Bott.

Collins, Suzanne. **Mockingjay**. *The Hunger Games*. Scholastic, 2010. 390p. $17.99. 978-0-439-02351-1. $22.99 PLB. 978-0-545-31060-4.
VOYA December 2010. **5Q · 5P · J/S** (SF/F/H)
Teens' Top Ten 2011.

If fervent fans of *The Hunger Games* trilogy (**The Hunger Games**, 2008; **Catching Fire**, 2009) were expecting **Mockingjay**, its final installment, to highlight Katniss's actions in the Capitol's destruction and finally choose Peeta or Gale amid peace and prosperity, jaws are instead dropping. Now in District 13, entirely underground and a secret base for the Capitol's nuclear weapons, Katniss is beautified and redesigned as a Mockingjay, Panem's symbol for justice. Outwardly, she must project herself as a fierce, glorious warrior for the next rebellion's morale and success, but inwardly she despises being District 13's pawn in their long-planned quest for the Capitol's power. She increasingly feels futility, seeing no victory in the Capitol usurped by an equally manipulative District.

An anguished Katniss again narrates, shattered by previous warfare and the understanding that all Districts contain victimized individuals. Searching for stability and purpose, she seeks advice from family and other familiar faces. Accustomed solace comes neither from Peeta, released from the Capitol's torture as a dangerous adversary, nor Gale, now a strident, single-minded rebel warrior.

The final battle is visceral, personal, and unspeakably cruel; many actions are shocking and unexpected, leaving readers and characters equally drained. Such particulars, however, should be arduous reading to validate the reality and effects of power, corruption, and resultant wars upon all, but especially their legacy to children, as revealed in the heartbreaking, hopeful epilogue. There the series comes full circle, illustrating the price Katniss paid as Prim's substitute in the original games, with that choice launching all subsequent events. Although overlong in places, this harsh, honest, and utterly compelling novel does not disappoint, purposefully requiring more thought concerning the story's messages than time spent in its reading.—Lisa Hazlett.

Coville, Bruce, Ed. **Half-Human**. Scholastic, 2004, ©2001. 224p. $5.99 Trade pb. 978-0-590-95588-1.

VOYA December 2001. **5Q · 5P · M · J · S** (SF/F/H)

Coville's choice short story collection, combining myth, magic, mystery, and characters "who are like us, but not quite" explores the wonder and challenge of identity, independence, love, and sacrifice. Coville joins Jane Yolen, Tamora Pierce, D. J. Malcolm, Jude Mandell, Janni Lee Simner, Nancy Springer, and Tim Waggoner, whose characters' journeys center on universal dilemmas. A tree transformed into a man overcomes the fear of fire to save a young woman who must masquerade as a boy or die in Pierce's *Elder Brother*. Four girls in separate stories-gorgon, dragon, selkie, and mermaid-decide how their inherited differences define them. In Greg Maguire's *Scarecrow*, a scarecrow leaves rumor behind to seek truth on the yellow brick road. A young girl and a young man in different tales reconcile the myths of the centaur and Icarus with their modern worlds. A centuries-old grandson gives Coville's *The Hardest, Kindest Gift*, mortality, to his grandmother, a fallen angel.

Defining theme and structure, Coville's introduction suggests booktalk approaches and classroom applications. Lawrence Schimel's poem "How to Make a Human," placed in the center of the collection, provocatively implies that humankind detached from nature is inept and destructive. Author information at the end of the collection includes suggestions for more fine reading. Theme and content parallel novels such as Donna Jo Napoli's **Sirena** (Scholastic, 1998/**VOYA** December 1998) and **Crazy Jack** (Delacorte, 1999/**VOYA** December 1998), Priscilla Galloway's **Snake Dreamer** (Delacorte, 1998/**VOYA** December 1998), and Katherine Roberts's **Spellfall** (Scholastic, 2001/**VOYA** December 2001) Although marketed for grades three to nine, this collection will captivate older young adult as well as adult readers, fantasy fans or not.—Lucy Schall.

Crist-Evans, Craig. **Amaryllis**. Candlewick, 2003. 184p. 978-0-7636-1863-6. O. P.

VOYA December 2003. **5Q · 5P · J**

In 1965, a large Greek freighting vessel, the Amaryllis, ran aground during a hurricane off the eastern coast of Florida and remained there for three years, a hulking beachside monstrosity. In Crist-Evans's story of life in Vietnam-era America, the huge ship becomes a metaphor for the war, for life with an abusive father, and for a Florida family's unbearable loss. Although Jimmy always admired the way his older brother, Frank, resisted their father's tyranny, he is devastated when Frank chooses the war in Vietnam as an opportunity for escape. As Jimmy attempts a typical teenage life, his emotional well-being is gradually worn down by the contents of Frank's letters detailing his experiences in Vietnam. As with most combat soldiers at that time, Frank is eventually overwhelmed by obscene events and relentless danger. After suffering a painful wound, Frank becomes addicted to heroin and soon loses all optimism about life or the likelihood that he will make it home alive. Eventually his letters stop, and the family is notified that Frank is missing in action.

Frank's experience as it unfolds in his letters feels very real, very complicated, and very tragic as does Jimmy's attempt to deal with his brother's problems from halfway around the world. The author accurately portrays the powerlessness felt by American families of Vietnam combat soldiers, as well as the senselessness of the war. Although war atrocities are implied, there is nothing graphic that would prevent middle school readers from reading it. Crist-Evans's book is engaging without being melodramatic and realistic without being unbearably disturbing.—James Blasingame."

Curtis, Christopher Paul. **Bucking the Sarge**. Wendy Lamb Books/Random House, 2004. 240p. PLB $17.99. 978-0-385-90159-8. $6.99 pb. 978-0-440-41331-8. **VOYA** October 2004. **5Q · 5P · J · S**
Top Ten Best Books for Young Adults 2005.

Newbery award-winning author Curtis aims for an older audience and hits a bull's-eye with this darker and uglier contemporary portrait of his native Flint, Michigan. Ninth-grader Luther T. Farrell loathes his greedy, loan-sharking, slumlord mother, known to everyone as "the Sarge," who milks the system to take advantage of disadvantaged, elderly, and low-income people. Even more loathsome is his mother's henchman/lover, Darnell Dixon, who has no compunction about breaking all the rules and forces Luther to do some of the dirty work. Luther's dream is to escape Flint forever, and winning his third science fair will put him on track for college. Luther gets the opportunity to break ties with his mother once and for all and expose her for the villain she is when his science project, about the effects of lead paint on the development of children, ties for first place. Luther's project prompts the mayor's office to launch a citywide investigation that means big trouble for the Sarge, who years ago fraudulently obtained and used lead paint for her properties. Infuriated, the Sarge tells Luther to pack his bags, but he finds her stash of hidden money, takes enough to pay for college, and heads down south to pursue his dream.

This superbly crafted story is populated by memorable quirky characters, such as Luther's best friend, Sparky, and his mysterious octogenarian roommate. As in Curtis's other novels, there is plenty of hilarity. At the core of the story, though, is Luther's profoundly inspiring determination to stay true to his values and to force his mother to answer for her many transgressions. No library should be without it.—Ed Sullivan.

Dashner, James. **The Scorch Trials**. *Maze Runner Trilogy*. Delacorte/Random House, 2010. 368p. $17.99. 978-0-385-73875-0. $20.99 PLB. 978-0-385-73875-0. **VOYA** December 2010. **5Q · 5P · J · S**
Thomas and the gladers thought they were safe. They thought they were glad to leave the danger of the maze far behind them. They were wrong. In one night, all their new-found security is ripped away, replaced by a new set of dangers: the Scorch, an area of land decimated by solar flares, brutal weather, and populated by the Cranks, people who are infected with a disease called the flare. Teresa is gone, in her place a boy who speaks of having survived another maze. Then a man appears telling them they have two weeks to travel one hundred miles of the Scorch to reach a safe haven, which will make escaping the maze look like child's play. **The Scorch Trials** is the second book in the trilogy that began with the best seller **The Maze Runner** (Random House, 2009/**VOYA** December 2009), picking up right where it left off.

Dashner writes at a suspenseful pace, weaving twists and turns into chapters that flow seamlessly together, culminating in a stunning cliff-hanger ending. Themes of moral dilemmas and survival amidst a deadly landscape make the danger even more chilling and heart-stopping. Readers will be on the edge of their seats with this thrilling story, and it is also makes a great match for fans of *The Hunger Games* trilogy by Suzanne Collins (Scholastic Press).—Susan Hampe.

Delsol, Wendy. **Stork**. Candlewick, 2010. 368p. $15.99. 978-0-7636-4844-2.
VOYA December 2010. **5Q · 5P · J · S**

After her parents' split, sixteen-year-old Katla and her mom leave sunny SoCal for her mom's hometown of Norse Falls, Minnesota. Kat misses her dad, trendy fashions, and Starbucks, but she's been given a good distraction: she's been tapped to join the ancient, secret, and select Icelandic Stork Society, in which she is not only the newest member but also the youngest to date. Taken under Fru Hulda's wing, Kat is learning more than how to guide the right unborn soul to the proper mother—she's also learning how to navigate more personal issues, like why Jack Snjosson, the close-mouthed, popular starting quarterback and editor of the school paper, seems mad that Kat does not remember him from childhood visits. Can one girl juggle the politics of the Stork Society, find new friends, and battle her crush on an angry young man with secrets while keeping secrets of her own? She can, if that girl is Kat.

Smart, funny, and so perfectly constructed, this book should go to the top of everyone's to-be-read pile. Kat has witty thoughts, in addition to droll dialogue, so the humor never feels forced or false and will even cause readers to laugh out loud. The clever story line has unexpected twists and a satisfying ending, with plenty of potential for future novels. The addition of a growing romance between our heroine and her hero, the well-developed background story of her parents' divorce and her mom starting over, and the possible revitalization of this small town just add to the depth of the story and the overall enjoyment each page of this book delivers.—Stacey Hayman..

Dessen, Sarah. **Just Listen**. Viking, 2006. 384p. $17.99. 978-0-670-06105-1. PLB $17.99. 978-1-4352-4975-2. $8.99 pb. 978-0-14-241097-4.
VOYA April 2006. **5Q · 5P · J · S**
Best Books for Young Adults 2007.
Teens' Top Ten 2007.

High school junior and part-time model Annabel hides her loneliness behind her beautiful face. Her friendship with manipulative, vengeful, but popular Sophie caused a rift with her best friend, Clarke. Now Sophie will not speak to her. What Sophie thought happened between Annabel and Will, Sophie's boyfriend, at last June's end-of-school party was not what really took place, but Annabel feels that she cannot tell anyone the truth. Her sister's anorexia is enough for her family to deal with. Sophie will not listen, and Clarke avoids her. On the first day of school, Annabel sits alone during lunch on the courtyard wall near outcast Owen, who was arrested for beating someone up. Obliviously listening to music every day, Owen soon becomes her friend. He sees past Annabel's façade, finding the real Annabel and expecting her to live up to her true self. When

Sophie's friend Emily, also a model, is accosted by Will, she files charges. Will it force Annabel to come to grips with her past and her present?

Dessen's books are engrossing, each one better than its predecessor, and her prose is smooth. Teens will relate to this story about a girl feeling isolated from family and friends. The characters are real-some quirky, some manipulative, some weak, some strong. Annabel's family dynamics will strike a familiar chord with many readers. Music is a major and welcome element in many of this author's works. Dessen weaves a sometimes funny, mostly emotional, and very satisfying story.—Ed Goldberg.

_____. **This Lullaby**. Viking, 2002. 352p. $16.99. 978-0-670-03530-4. PLB $16.99. 978-1-4352-8734-1. $8.99 pb. 978-0-14-250155-9.
VOYA June 2002. **5Q · 5P · J · S**
Best Books for Young Adults 2003.

Although eighteen-year-old Remy's father left her mother before she was born and died soon after he went away, his ghost haunts Remy in the form of a hit song he wrote, "This Lullaby." Penned in honor of her birth, the ballad becomes a schmaltzy hit played on lite-rock radio and during father $ND daughter dances at weddings. Remy hates the song and the intimacy it implies; to the obsessively organized Remy, intimacy is something to be avoided. As Remy plans her mother's fifth wedding, she anticipates her freshman year at Stanford where she can finally enjoy the distance she craves. When Remy meets Dexter, lead singer of a traveling rock band, the depth of their relationship threatens to disrupt her strategy for a no-strings summer before her escape to California.

As Dessen's body of work expands, her novels deepen. With its deceptively simple summer romance plot, this book documents adolescent life with perception and acuity. Remy, her family, and friends are unique and fully realized characters with complementing story lines. Not one for typecasting, Dessen creates characters with unapologetic faults and no moralizing. Remy and her friends, like many teenagers, occasionally drink, smoke, and ponder sex; however, these activities and musings are not fodder for narrative sermonizing. The decisions the teens make-although real-do not carry with them the obvious repercussions present in a more cautionary tale. With Dessen's sympathy, accuracy, and genuine respect for her characters and readers, this novel is sure to become another favorite of high school readers.—Amy S. Pattee.

_____. **What Happened to Goodbye**. Viking, 2011. 402p. $19.99. 978-0-670-01294-7.
VOYA June 2011. **5Q · 5P · J · S**
Best Fiction for Young Adults 2012.
Readers' Choice 2012.

Dessen scores a three-pointer with this skillfully written novel about family and starting over. Mclean and her father, a restaurant consultant, move around a lot because of his job after she chooses him over her mother. Her mom cheated on her dad in the most hurtful way possible and ruined his passion—basketball—for him forever. Because of this, Mclean is very protective of her father. Moving all of the time allows

Mclean to reinvent herself over and over again. She is able to hide from herself. The problem is that she never has the chance to make friends and settle into her life. This is just fine with her; roots hurt too much when they are ripped out. With the latest move, things could change—whether Mclean likes it or not.

Dessen's prose is clean and focused, the characters are developed and real, and the plot is believable. Mclean's journey through the healing process after her parents' divorce provides bibliotherapy for any teen dealing with family issues, and the secondary plot of tentative steps toward trust and friendship is beautiful. This is a must-have for any young adult collection.—Kristina Weber.

Dogar, Sharon. **Annexed: The Powerful Story of the Boy Who Loved Anne Frank**. Houghton Mifflin Harcourt, 2010. 352p. $17. 978-0-547-50195-6. Further Reading.
VOYA October 2010. **5Q · 5P · J · S**

In this imaginary tale, Dogar presents the heartbreaking story of Peter van Pels, the boy who fell in love with Anne Frank. When Peter enters the Annex in 1942, he is almost sixteen, almost a man. Plagued with nightmares and frightening thoughts, Peter seeks solace in the attic where he can see a little piece of sky. As he watches the seasons pass, Peter goes through a whirlwind of emotions contemplating why Jews are hated, why is he hiding instead of fighting, why he should survive when so many are dying. At first, Peter finds Anne to be an annoyingly chatty child who is always insulting him and behaves as if their predicament is a "house party." Over time, Peter finds great comfort in Anne's company as he begins to notice her scent, her changing shape as she becomes a woman, and that he enjoys making her smile.

Annexed stands out as one of the best books published this year and is a must-purchase for all public and school library collections. Dogar's writing is poetic and gripping, drawing the reader deep into Peter's story. Peter's emotions are raw and honestly portrayed; he is a teenage boy facing death, scared that he will never get to do something as simple as make love to a woman. Even though the ending has been foretold, Dogar adds a new layer to the story through Peter, whose voice is hauntingly accurate. Going beyond the betrayal in the annex, Dogar explores what daily life would have been like for Peter in Auschwitz and does a fabulous job of imagining Peter's tale while keeping Anne Frank's story and the historical facts intact. Readers do not need to read **The Diary of Anne Frank** to enjoy **Annexed**, though it serves as an excellent companion novel and a wonderful addition to Holocaust literature for teens.—Sarah Cofer.

Donnelly, Jennifer. **Revolution**. Delacorte/Random House, 2010. 496p. $18.99. 978-0-385-73763-0. PLB $21.99. 978-0-385-90678-4.
VOYA December 2010. **5Q · 5P · S**
Top Ten Best Fiction for Young Adults 2011.
Popular Paperbacks for Young Adults 2013.

The book begins with Andi and some of her classmates at the weekly Friday morning breakfast party, where each gets high in her or his own way before heading to school.

Oh, no! Not another teen-angst tale! While it is that, it is so much more. Andi Alpers is a senior at St. Anselm's, a prestigious private school in Brooklyn, New York. Her seven-year-old brother, Truman, was killed in a traffic accident two years earlier, and Andi blames herself because she was supposed to be looking after him. She lives with her artist mother in an apartment, and her father, a Nobel-prize-winning geneticist who left after his son's death, is now involved with a much younger woman. Andi's grades have slipped in all her classes except music, which, along with antidepressants, is her escape. She has managed to keep her academic and emotional problems from her mother, who is suffering in her own way, continually painting portraits of Truman. Andi arrives home one evening to find her father waiting for her. He has his wife admitted to a psychiatric hospital and informs Andi that she will be accompanying him to Paris for her winter break and working on the outline for her senior thesis. In Paris, Andi is given an old guitar which contains diary that belonged to Alexandrine Paradis, daughter of a family of entertainers. As Andi becomes engrossed in the diary, she becomes more and more interested not only in doing research for her thesis about an eighteenth-century French composer named Amadé Malherbeau but also in a young French musician she meets in a club.

This relatively hefty volume might not work for the readers of Lurlene McDaniel, but give it to those who love Gregory Maguire or Libba Bray.—Marlyn Beebe.

Earls, Nick. **48 Shades of Brown**. Graphia/Houghton Mifflin, 2004, ©1999. 288p. $7.99 Trade pb. 978-0-618-45295-8.

VOYA April 2004. **5Q · 5P · S**

Named Australia's Children's Book Council 2000 Book of the Year for Older Readers, this enchanting coming-of-age novel is both hilarious and touching. Intelligent and sheltered Dan (a.k.a. Banger), the sixteen-year-old narrator, decides to complete his final school year in Australia. His parents will be in Geneva, Switzerland. He will live with his Aunt Jacq, a recent university graduate, and Naomi, her beautiful, flighty housemate, a university student a few years older than Dan. The situation presents practical responsibilities and his own sexual awakening. Expectations for cooking and cleaning confound him. His amorous feelings for Naomi dominate his life and lead him to use his intellectual powers for girl appeal. Dan's academic, housekeeping, and romantic roles combine and climax at a university party in which he and his friend plan to get girls by passing themselves off as second year law students. He learns a hard lesson instead: Drunks vomit. In the party fallout, Jacq reveals that she also holds amorous feelings for Naomi, Naomi discovers a new male lover, and Dan decides that he might have a chance with the girl he fooled at the party who was also posing as a university student.

With small details about throwing up, basil, Romeo and Juliet, brown birds, postcards, and sex, Earls builds a too-true story that neither older young adults nor adults will be able to put down as their smiles become belly laughs that lead them to new perspectives.—Lucy Schall.

Ellis, Deborah. **We Want You to Know: Kids Talk about Bullying**. Coteau, 2010. 120p. $21.95 Trade pb. 978-1-55050-417-0.

VOYA December 2010. **5Q · 5P · M · J · S · A/YA** (NF)

Ellis's words are minimal as she lets fearful, tortured, powerless, and reclaimed voices speak about their painful experiences. Each chapter begins with a brief introduction followed by personal stories of those who have been bullied, as well as a few who were bullies. These young people believe the school staff did little to help protect them, and the antibullying assemblies and programs did not change the environment. Each section ends with "What Do You Think?" questions, and sidebars highlight statements from kids around the world: Angola, California, Japan, Singapore, South Korea, Sri Lanka, Uganda, and more.

This book can be used with all young people and adults, as it deals with a problem that touches all of us and seems to evade solutions. So many emotions rise from these pages that the reader cannot remain untouched. Subaru Yokota from Japan assigns us all a mission to act: "You must embrace courage and have absolute determination that you are going to stop bullying. You can't just see the prey get hunted by the predator. You have to stop it. You have to be heroes."—C. J. Bott.

Emond, Stephen. **Winter Town**. Little, Brown, 2011. 336p. $17.99. 978-0-316-13332-6.

VOYA April 2012. **5Q · 5P · J · S**

Since childhood, Lucy and Evan have been best friends. They had been the "happy wanderers" in their New England town, combining their talents to create an imaginary world with a vomiting yellow sun. When they were twelve years old, Lucy's parents split up, and Lucy moved with her mom to Atlanta, only to return annually for the week encompassing Christmas and New Year's Day. This year, they are both seventeen. Evan is mired in college preparation. Lucy arrives with dark hair and a nose piercing, radiating abject misery. The friends have a week to assemble and reassemble their relationship, even as they struggle to face their individual futures.

Emond gives such deep, insightful glimpses into the minds and hearts of these two teens that it is easy to forget he is writing in third person. The intimacy of Lucy and Evan is palpable in all the ways they easily become the duo of their childhood, but it is also very clear that their comfortable roles do not really fit their nearly-adult selves. This lovely, character-driven novel is enhanced by the author's illustrations. Many of these are Evan's cartoons, loaded with the emotions he cannot express. Other drawings depict the snow-covered "real" world, where Evan and Lucy clumsily search for themselves and each other. The stark winter beauty portrayed in the illustrations contributes to a mood of bittersweet loneliness, perfectly capturing the comfort and constraints of childhood rituals. Recommend this for teens who appreciate well-crafted realistic fiction and for fans of graphic novels who enjoy a story extended through artwork.—Diane Colson.

Evanovich, Janet and Alex Evanovich. **Troublemaker**, Book 1. Dark Horse Books, 2010. 112p. $17.99. 978-1-59582-488-2.

Evanovich, Janet and Alex Evanovich. **Troublemaker**, Book 2. Dark Horse Books, 2010. 112p. $17.99. 978-1-59582-573-5.

VOYA February 2011. **5Q · 5P · A/YA** (G)

The *Troublemaker* stories feature Barnaby and Hooker from Evanovich's previous books, **Metro Girl** (HarperTorch, 2004) and **Motor Mouth** (HarperCollins, 2006). Alex Barnaby, a mechanic for NASCAR driver, Sam Hooker, discovers a ransom note for her friend, Felicia, along with a voodoo doll. Barnaby immediately wants to call the police. Instead, she is manipulated into looking for Felicia with Hooker. Trouble follows them as they are chased by people in boats and cars, while also escaping bombings and deadly snakes. Amidst the danger, they uncover clues to Felicia's whereabouts. The first book ends on a cliff-hanger but the second installment picks up the story immediately.

Set in New Orleans, the setting of **Troublemaker Book 1** rings true through swamp exploits, voodoo experts, and the city's well known nightlife. **Troublemaker Book 2** takes place in Florida and New Orleans. The colorful, engaging art compliments the text and adds depth and humor to the story. The panels are easy to follow, making it accessible for adults unaccustomed to reading graphic novels. For teens not familiar with Evanovich's work, these will be a great introduction to her novels. As with Evanovich's novels, action and danger fuel the story, with humor and a touch of romance thrown in for good measure.—Jennifer Rummel.

Fantaskey, Beth. **Jessica's Guide to Dating on the Dark Side**. Houghton Mifflin Harcourt, 2009. 368p. $17. 978-0-15-206384-9. $8.99 pb. 978-0-547-25940-6.

VOYA June 2009. **5Q · 5P · J · S** (SF/F/H)

When Lucius Vladescu arrives to collect his long-lost, betrothed Romanian vampire princess, Anastasia Dragomir, he finds in her place American teen Jessica Packwood. Jessica is a mathlete and member of 4-H, raised by vegan, anthropologist parents who brought her to America. She knows very little about her birth parents and her brief life as Anastasia, and she likes it that way. What she does know is that she is certainly not an undead vampire princess, especially if it means being betrothed to the arrogant, overbearing, and dangerous Lucius. But Jessica finds that there is much at stake should the pact between the Vladescus and Dragomirs be broken; there is a vampire war brewing in Romania, and Lucius's very life may depend on Jessica's decision. Will she leave her "nice," rational life with her best friend Mindy and boyfriend Jake, or will she accept her destiny and ascend to the throne as Anastasia Dragomir?

Fantaskey's novel is far more than a romantic fantasy. As Jessica wrestles with issues of identity, she must also grapple with her body's physical changes and her newfound sexuality. For answers, she turns to "Growing Up Undead: A Teen Vampire's Guide to Dating, Health, and Emotions," a title that reveals vampirism as the novel's metaphor for coming-of-age. Jessica is a witty, spunky protagonist with authentic insecurities and inner conflicts.—Courtney Huse Wika.

Fleming, Candace. **The Great and Only Barnum: The Tremendous, Stupendous Life of Showman P. T. Barnum**. Schwartz and Wade, 2009. 160p. $18.99. 978-0-375-84197-2. PLB $21.99. 978-0-375-94597-7. Index. Illus. Photos. Biblio. Source Notes.
VOYA August 2009. **5Q · 5P · M · J · S** (NF)
Nonfiction Award Finalist 2010.
Best Books for Young Adults 2010.

Abandon all preconceived notions about P. T. Barnum, ye who enter here. Settle down and enjoy this delightful, illuminating, illustrated biography of one of America's more fascinating characters. Fleming tells the riveting story of showman Barnum, who invented aquariums, reinvented museums and circuses, never stopped working, bounced back from numerous catastrophes—bankruptcy, total business losses from fire—and was a surprisingly hardworking public servant whose agile intellect also found pleasure in hosting a popular literary salon. Fleming's work is rich in photographs, engravings, and frequent sidebars that add texture to the flavor of the American psyche that was ripe for what Barnum was offering. She puts into perspective the attraction for human curiosities (bearded women, skeleton men, Tom Thumb, Chang and Eng) during the nineteenth century, a practice that is rightfully repugnant by today's standards.

Barnum's ability to think outside the box time and again is a study in entrepreneurship. He thrived on risk-taking and rarely failed. Although he was a self-admitted humbugger, fooling his audiences with hoaxes, he was so good-natured about it that they clamored for more. Fleming offers a terrific accessible insider's view of an important piece of America's cultural and entertainment history.—Beth E. Andersen.

Forman, Gayle. **Where She Went**. Dutton/Penguin, 2011. 208p. $16.99. 978-0-525-42294-5.
VOYA June 2011. **5Q · 5P · S**
Readers' Choice 2012.
Popular Paperbacks for Young Adults 2013.
Best Fiction for Young Adults 2012.

Forman's sequel begins three years after her fine novel **If I Stay** (Dutton/Penguin, 2009/**VOYA** February 2009) concludes. Mia has recovered from the devastating automobile crash that killed her parents and brother, has finished her studies as a cellist at Julliard, and is about to embark upon her first world concert tour. What she has not managed to take care of very well is the young man left in the wake of her climb back to a normal life—Adam. A talented musician in his own right, Adam sat by Mia's side at the hospital and even moved into her grandparents' home once she was out of rehab, coaxing her toward better health—that is, until Mia left for New York and, within weeks, cut him off without explanation or apology. Mentally crushed and adrift, Adam turns his raw feelings into two cathartic rock albums that send his band into superstardom. The initial charge of the celebrity life burns out quickly for Adam, however. When the novel opens, he is on the brink of a complete breakdown. Then circumstances cause Mia's and Adam's lives to intersect for a single evening in New York City.

Told from Adam's point of view—one laced with cynicism, desperation, and exhaustion—Forman's tale is pitch-perfect. Here she deals with the long-term aftermath of tragedy and the difficulty of recovery. A path from illness to health seems straightforward, but as Forman deftly describes, it is very complicated and wrought with anger, guilt, pity, and blame. The injured were not just those in the car but also those that surround Mia—and Adam. Arguably, Forman has succeeded at an even more difficult objective than set forth in the first book. Forman's prose will adequately carry those who pick up Where She Went without the benefit of the pre-story, but they will miss the full beauty of Adam and Mia's tale if they do not start at the beginning. The set is greater than the sum of its parts—an absolute must-buy for collections serving teens.—Lauri J. Vaughan.

Fredericks, Mariah. **The True Meaning of Cleavage**. Atheneum/S & S, 2003. 224p. 978-0-689-85092-9. O.P.
VOYA April 2003. **5Q · 5P · M · J**
Teens Top Ten 2003.

Jess, into science fiction and art, and Sari, into clothes and boys, are best friends. Barely settled into their freshman year at a New York City alternative school, Sari sets her sights on David, the senior jock who already has the perfect girlfriend. Sari is obsessed and will do anything to be David's girl, beginning with a sexual encounter in the bathroom at a party. Their secret meetings escalate to weekly sex at David's house. Sari cannot see that she is being used, until in desperation she tries to force David to acknowledge her at a party, and he walks away.

The title certainly rings true. Sari painfully realizes that the seductive hollow separating her breasts might attract a guy's attention, but it can also be a visual reminder of the broken heart beneath. Jess discovers that slowly growing into her body and into a relationship with a guy is more her style. Most important, no matter what issues temporarily separate Jess and Sari, they will always be best friends in this must-read for every middle and junior high school girl. With Jess as the narrator, the message is clear, but it is not told in sexually graphic terms. Jess's sense of humor and her obsession with an upcoming science fiction movie will have teens chuckling as they keep reading to find out what out-of-control thing Sari will do next. Fredericks creates a modern day **Forever** that should escape the censor's sword.—Ruth E. Cox.

Frost, Helen. **Hidden**. Farrar, Straus, Giroux/Macmillan, 2011. 160p. $16.99. 978-0-374-38221-6.
VOYA June 2011. **5Q · 5P · J**
Quick Pick Nomination 2012.

When Wren was eight years old, she was accidentally kidnapped while she was in the back of her parent's minivan at a gas station. The kidnapper did not know she was in the car, as Wren kept quiet. His daughter, Darra, figured it out, though, and left food for her once the van was hidden away inside her garage. A few years later, Wren and Darra meet again at Camp Oakwood in Michigan. Darra's father is gone, and she blames Wren for it. Wren lives through the terror of being kidnapped once again when she sees

Darra—all the memories that were tucked away come flooding back. She leaves an un-signed note for Darra: "If you don't talk about who I was or how you knew me, I won't talk about you or your dad."

The story is told using a combination of poetry and prose. Frost is a master at letting each girl's feelings unfold from when they were eight and when they meet again. She leads them through a believable path of discovery about themselves and the people in their lives that they love. Teen readers will be intrigued by the kidnapping that opens the story, which is told at a fast pace through straightforward poems. They will likely want to follow Wren later in life. Many teen readers will identify with Wren and Darra and how events that happened to us when we were younger help shape the person we become.—K. Czarnecki.

_____. **Keesha's House**. Frances Foster Books/Farrar Straus Giroux, 2003. 128p. $16. 978-0-374-34064-3. $8.99 pb. 978-0-374-40012-5.
VOYA April 2003. **5Q · 5P · M · J · S**
Michael L. Printz Honor 2004.

Keesha's house with its blue door is really Joe's-a haven for lost and unwanted teens in trouble, offering shelter, safety, and sober comfort when the loving home for which one wishes just is not happening. Compelling first-person accounts by and about seven bewildered teens grip the reader. Using the traditional poetic forms of sestine and sonnet-whose rules are largely followed but occasionally broken with careful intent and fully explained at the end-Frost's debut young adult novel succeeds beyond this English teacher's imagination. Sentences wrapping from one stanza into the next draw readers through stories that embrace all the uncertainty and fear of teen life when adults' failures force the teens into early maturity. Told in eight sections, their stories touch on issues of race, class, and residence; encompass pregnancy, responsibility, addiction, homosexual-ity, abuse, neglect, abandonment, and delinquency; and still leave room for the voices of peripheral adults. With personal problems galore, these teenagers still find ways to reach out and help others in need.

Spare, eloquent, and elegantly concise, Frost's novel will reach reluctant readers as well as those drawn to **Go Ask Alice** or work by Walter Dean Myers, Nancy Garden, Carolyn Coman, or Ann M. Martin. Public, private, or correctional educators and li-brarians should put this must-read on their shelves. Already an accomplished poet and prolific children's nonfiction author, Frost has found another genre that suits her well.—Cynthia Winfield.

Funke, Cornelia. **Igraine the Brave**. The Chicken House/Scholastic, 2007. 224p. $16.99. 978-0-439-90379-0.
VOYA December 2007. **5Q · 5P · M · J** (SF/F/H)

Fantasy fans looking for a spunky, adventurous new heroine will find one in this new novel from Funke. Igraine, a twelve-year-old who wants nothing more than to be-come a knight, is surrounded by those who care little for adventure or swordplay. Her parents, The Fair Melisande and Sir Lamorak the Wily, are the keepers of the Singing Books of Magic and two of the most powerful magicians in the land. Her brother, Albert, is studying to follow in their footsteps. Igraine, however, has little interest in magic and no talent for remembering spells. Unfortunately she also has little opportunity to practice her knightly skills. Pimpernel Castle is well defended by her family's magic, although no one has attacked in many years. But when a greedy new neighbor makes plans to seize the Singing Books and a magical mistake leaves the castle's defenses weakened and Igraine's family in danger, she must use every bit of her skill and courage and even some magic to save her home.

Fun characters and illustrations by the author create a light fantasy adventure in the spirit of T. H. White's **The Sword in the Stone** (Collins, 1938). Albert is a talented older brother, who frequently likes to tease his tomboy sister, and Igraine's parents seem silly and absent minded, but when faced with a real threat, the brave Igraine and her family work together and show their true strength. Funke's book will be a hit with all young fantasy fans.—Anita Beaman.

Gagnon, Michelle. **Don't Turn Around**. HarperCollins, 2012. 320p. $17.99. 978-0-06-210290-4.
VOYA August 2012. **5Q · 5P · M · J · S**

Teens all around the world are dying of PEMA, a mysterious and incurable wasting disease. Noa and Peter are two teens with advanced hacking skills but radically different backgrounds. Peter is a rich kid who started /ALLIANCE/, an online group of hackers, and Noa (reminiscent of *Dragon Tattoo*'s Lisbeth Salander) is a former foster kid who has gone off the grid, making money under an assumed identity by testing and setting up website and company security. The two teens are brought together when Peter starts poking around one of his father's business interests. This leads to a home invasion by "men in black" type goons who take his laptop and threaten him. Noa wakes up on a metal operating table with an incision in her chest, strapped to an IV, and wearing only a cloth gown. She barely escapes and goes on the run. After tapping into some money she has saved, she gets a new computer which puts her into contact with both Peter and the mysterious A6M0 who warns her when she is in danger. Realizing they are both being chased by the same people, and that it has something to do with PEMA research, they start working together to figure out what is going on and what was done to Noa and why.

This fast-paced thriller will keep all readers, including adults, on the edge of their seats. This is a must-purchase title, especially for libraries looking for something besides the paranormal. Be prepared to stay up all night reading; the ending can stand alone or support a sequel.—Suanne B. Roush.

Gaiman, Neil. **Coraline**. Adapted and illus. by P. Craig Russell. HarperCollins, 2008. 192p. $18.99. 978-0-06-082543-0. $9.99 pb. 978-0-06-082545-4.
VOYA June 2008. **5Q · 5P · M · J** (SF/F/H)

Russell adds new dimension to **Coraline** (HarperCollins, 2002/**VOYA** October 2002) in this delightfully creepy graphic novel adaptation of Gaiman's bestseller, faithfully retelling the story of a bored girl who discovers a magical and dangerous parallel world through a door in her family's large, old house. At first, Coraline is excited by the marvels of this strange new world, including her "Other Mother." But Coraline soon realizes that there is something sinister about the Other Mother, who looks like her real mother, except for her black button eyes and long sharp fingernails. The Other Mother wants to replace Coraline's eyes with buttons, too, so she can stay in her new home "for ever and always." When Coraline returns to her world, she discovers that her parents are trapped in a shadowy prison behind a hallway mirror. With the enigmatic help of a talking black cat, Coraline gathers her courage and goes off to face the Other Mother and win her parents' freedom.

Fans of Gaiman's tale will embrace Russell's vision and appreciate the compelling way in which the text and illustrations complement each other. Russell's artwork powerfully evokes both the wonder and terror of the Other Mother's realm. The illustrations also bring new depth to the supporting characters, including Coraline's eccentric neighbors and the black cat that comes across as both annoying and lovable. This adaptation is also a great way to introduce readers to Gaiman's work and an appealing choice for reluctant readers.—Amy Luedtke.

Gantos, Jack. **Joey Pigza Loses Control**. Farrar Straus Giroux, 2002, ©2000. 196p. $5.99 pb. 978-0-06-441022-9.
VOYA February 2001. **5Q · 5P · M · J**
Newbery Award 2001.

In this sequel to **Joey Pigza Swallowed the Key** (Farrar Straus Giroux, 1998/**VOYA** February 1999), Joey begins his visit with his father on a relatively even keel because of the medication he takes to treat his attention deficit hyperactivity disorder (ADHD). It is not, however, an easy father-and-son reunion, as Carter Pigza is an adult version of the non-medicated Joey, so wired that "a humming sound comes out of his body." Joey pitches for the baseball team that his father coaches, and Carter has plans for a winning season. Joey handles the demanding role of being the hotshot pitcher-son of the coach until Carter decides that Joey is a normal kid who does not need "crutches" and flushes Joey's medicine down the toilet. Although he wants to believe in his father, Joey knows that it will not be long before the old wired Joey comes back.

The reader is drawn into Joey's struggle for self-control while his medication wears off and as his father's behavior becomes more erratic with the increased consumption of alcohol. Through Joey's narration, Gantos brilliantly portrays the often-manic pace of an ADHD mind, but he alleviates the tension with touches of humor. Joey accidentally pierces his Chihuahua Pablo's ear with a wayward dart and wants to put an earring in the hole. His mother is not amused, although the reader cannot help but smile at Joey's antics. Joey is a young teen struggling to maintain control in an often out-of-control world, a struggle with which many teens will relate. Gantos's style of writing and the subject matter make this book a great middle school read-aloud.—Ruth Cox.

_____. **What Would Joey Do?** Farrar Straus Giroux, 2002. 240p. $16.99. 978-0-374-39986-3. PLB $14.99. 978-1-4395-1107-7. $5.99 pb. 978-0-06-054403-4.
VOYA December 2002. **5Q · 5P · M · J · S**

Joey Pigza is a well-meaning, lovable pre-teen with Attention Deficit Hyperactivity Disorder (ADHD). Joey and his mother are trying to get their lives back on track, but that might not be possible when Carter Pigza is around. Joey's father has roared back into town on a motorcycle, determined to lure his separated wife back into the chaotic whirlwind of his own unmedicated, unemployed ADHD lifestyle. In contrast to his father, Joey is smart and self-aware and has come a long way toward managing his erratic impulses. When Joey's mother starts spinning out of control in response to Carter's antics, the household's fragile stability quickly unravels. Joey also is being homeschooled by the devout Mrs. Lapp, whose blind daughter, Olivia, antagonizes her schoolmates so that her mother will give up homeschooling and send her to a school for the blind. Boosted by his dying grandmother's wish to see him make a friend, Joey's do-good intentions and ingenuity are stretched to hilarious and exasperating limits as he attempts to befriend the prickly Olivia. Joey's self-awareness training-to think before speaking and acting-intersect with Mrs. Lapp's favorite pronouncement, "What Would Jesus Do?" to blend into the new mantra, "What Would Joey Do?" What Joey does, despite the follies of his parents and numerous adversities, is quite remarkable.

This funny, heartwarming novel fully measures up to the acclaimed earlier adventures of the hyperactive hero in **Joey Pigza Swallowed the Key** (Farrar Straus Giroux, 1998/**VOYA** February 1999) and **Joey Loses Control** (2000/**VOYA** February 2001).—Walter Hogan.

Garcia, Kami, and Margaret Stohl. **Beautiful Darkness**. *Beautiful Creatures*. Little, Brown, 2010. 512p. 978-0-316-09861-8. O.P.
VOYA December 2010. **5Q · 5P · J · S** (SF/F/H)
Morris Award Finalist 2010.

Grief stricken after her Uncle Macon's death, Lena withdraws, unresponsive to Ethan's overtures, and drops out of school, becoming more and more reclusive. As Lena retreats, Ethan turns to Liv, Marian's new assistant at the library. When Ethan discovers Lena hanging out with Incubus John Breed, he fears he has lost her. Ethan confronts her at Ravenwood and discovers that her grandmother intends to take Lena away, but Lena and John sneak out and head for the Great Barrier, where neither light nor dark exist. When Sarafine calls a Claiming Moon out of time, Ethan, Link, and Liv follow Lena and John into the tunnels beneath Gatlin, determined to save Lena from becoming a Dark Caster. Ethan's mother appears to tell Ethan that Macon is not actually dead, and Ethan releases Macon from an Archlight where he has been trapped. Their fight for Lena's salvation results in casualties and consequences.

The authors ground their Caster world in the concrete, skillfully juxtaposing the arcane, magical world with Gatlin's normal southern lifestyle. Confused and vulnerable, Ethan demands our attention. His resolve to save Lena in this battle against supernatural powers is poignant. There is no happy ending, as the scene is deftly set for a sequel. The resulting conflict leaves Lena neither dark nor light, but part of both. Back in Gatlin, Ethan attempts to bury the Archlight in Macon's grave, but Ridley steals it. Link, bitten by a Blood Incubus, begins to transform. Fans will devour this latest book and plead for more.—Nancy K. Wallace.

Gier, Kerstin. **Sapphire Blue (Ruby Red)**. Henry Holt/Macmillan, 2012. 368p. $16.99. 978-0-8050-9266-0.
VOYA October 2012. **5Q · 5P · M · J · S**

Three days after being declared the Ruby, Gwen worries that the more she learns the less she knows. Adding to the confusion is her time-traveling companion, Gideon, a dashing young man who distracts her with kisses. Gwen is not sure if Gideon's feelings are real or if he is meant to divert her attention away from the mysterious Circle of Twelve, Count Saint-Germain, the Florentine Alliance, or reasons for Lucy and Paul's behavior. Gwen is hiding secrets of her own, like talking to ghosts and meeting her grandfather in the past, but she would gladly share information if somebody else—preferably Gideon—would do the same. Instead the only solid advice she's gotten is "Trust no one!"

This reader only has two complaints: (1) the book ended, and (2) waiting for **Emerald Green** is already straining her patience! Gwen is the best kind of reluctant, klutzy heroine; she—and others—underestimate her inherent smarts and skills until she triumphs over adversity, again. Gideon also has moments of feeling flawed and insecure, allowing him to be likable despite his wide-ranging talents and dreamy looks. Surrounded by quirky, lovable extras—including the ghost of a gargoyle—the whole gang grows dearer to the heart with every passing page. It is possible to begin with this second in a trilogy, but not necessary. Returning fans will be thrilled by more dashing swordplay, hints for decoding the prophecies, and plenty of flirty, romantic feelings. A satisfying cliff-hanger awaits readers at the end of this story.—Stacey Hayman.

Giles, Gail. **What Happened to Cass McBride?** Little, Brown, 2006. 224p. $16.99. 978-0-316-16638-6. $7.99 pb. 978-0-316-16639-3.
VOYA December 2006. **5Q · 5P · S**
Best Books for Young Adults 2007.
Top Ten Quick Picks for Reluctant Young Adult Readers 2007.

Kyle's dorky younger brother, David, a high school junior, has hanged himself. Grieving, Kyle pins the blame on David's classmate, Cass. She is Ms. Popularity, barely aware of David's existence, and Kyle chooses to believe that she sent David over the edge when she rebuffed him for a date. Bent on vengeance, Kyle kidnaps Cass, buries her in a box, and rigs up a speaking tube so that he can torture her with words while she dies. But thanks to a driven father who has taught Cass to be a "closer," words are Cass's weapon also. While the police race the clock to find her, Cass lures Kyle into a dialogue that causes them both to see themselves, their families, and David's death from fresh perspectives. But will Kyle's new insights influence him enough to spare Cass?

The story unfolds in alternating mini chapters from three points of view: Kyle's, Cass's, and the lead detective's. The structure makes for a choppy beginning, but the grisly subject matter compels, and the need to know Cass's destiny-life or death-will keep readers turning pages. Over and above plot, however, and intertwined with Cass's fate, are complex issues of responsibility and scapegoating that even the most black-and-white thinkers will ponder long after they close the book. Did just one factor cause

David's death? Were there others? If so, how should they be weighted and how, if appropriate, should punishment be meted out? To whom? By whom? Often brutal, this outstanding psychological thriller is recommended for older teens.—Mary E. Heslin.

GirlSource Editorial Team. **GirlSource: A Book by and for Young Women About Relationships, Rights, Futures, Bodies, Minds, and Souls**. Ten Speed Press, 2003. 96p. Trade pb. 978-1-58008-555-7. O.P. Index. Illus. Photos.
VOYA February 2004. **5Q · 5P · M · J · S** (NF)

This book is definitely the one that every teenage girl has been waiting for! In the new updated version of **It's About Time!** (GirlSource, 2000), the GirlSource editorial team takes every question today's young women might have and answers them in a no-holds-barred fashion. The topics covered include everything from stress, meditation, and depression to sex, STDs, and birth control; from rape and drugs to teens' rights with police; and from relationships and family issues to preparing for college.

Every topic is dealt with in an open and honest fashion that will be refreshing for teens. Best of all, the information in this book has not been filtered through adult eyes but comes straight from young women themselves. The GirlSource team surveyed more than five hundred young women from the San Francisco area on what were the most important issues for them. The result of all the surveys and research is a must-have book that will be the new number-one information source for young women. All public and school librarians should do their students the favor of having plenty of copies of this title on their shelves. Young women everywhere will thank you.—Lori Matthews.

Grant, Michael. **Fear**. *A Gone Novel*. Katherine Tegen/HarperCollins, 2012. 576p. $17.99. 978-0-06-144915-4.
VOYA October 2011. **5Q · 5P · J · S**

It has been four months of relative peace in the FAYZ. The killing flu is over, the supersized bugs are gone, and the remaining kids have divided themselves between living under Sam's council at Lake Tramonto or at Perdido Beach with King Caine. Regardless of location or leader, they have all found some degree of success in the everyday struggle for survival. When a dark stain begins to creep upward in multiple locations on the barrier wall, both camps realize this could be the final, fatal blow. If the stain closes out all the daylight, how will kids without a "Sammy sun" keep safe? More importantly, without sunshine, how will anything grow?

As the fifth entry in a series of six books, it is a relief to have a few of the original puzzles solved, but the solutions are not absolutely complete, and new queries are ready to take their place. One of the most satisfying revelations is discovering what has been happening outside the dome, but it raises deeper questions about life before the FAYZ. Most threatening moments in the story come from elements beyond the kids' control, giving a bleaker, more desperate aspect to their actions. Adding a layer of tension is the underlying feeling that judgment day is drawing near, but who will be judge and who will be jury? Fans can count on more excellent storytelling, multidimensional characters who continue to develop in unexpected ways, and some mighty fine eye-popping moments. Just how will readers manage to wait for Light?—Stacey Hayman.

_____. **Hunger**. *A Gone Novel.* HarperTeen, 2009. 608p. $17.99. 978-0-06-144906-2. PLB $18.89. 978-0-06-144907-9. $9.99 Trade pb. 978-0-06-144908-6.
VOYA June 2009. **5Q · 5P · M · J · S** (SF/F/H)

It is three months after everyone fifteen or older has vanished, and youth in the FAYZ (Fallout Alley Youth Zone) are barely surviving. Food is extremely scarce, and the young people are reduced to eating random canned goods, garbage, and at least one neighborhood pet. Sam is beginning to cave under the pressure of being in charge, and it is only getting worse as the general population becomes more apathetic about working toward their own survival. Conflict between the norms (normal youth) and the moofs (mutant freaks) escalates until there is an attempted lynching. The mysterious Darkness, naming itself a gaiaphage, is growing stronger, and it is working on a plan toward ultimate dominance of the FAYZ, but it needs a fuel rod from the nuclear power plant to succeed. Unable to break his connection from the gaiaphage, Caine attempts to appease it by taking the power plant from Sam and his people, but can either boy claim a victory if the Darkness gets what it needs?

Readers will be unable to avoid involuntarily gasping, shuddering, or flinching while reading this suspense-filled story. The tension starts in the first chapter and does not let up until the end. Some of the questions from **Gone** (HarperTeen, 2008/**VOYA** April 2008) are answered, but they leave new questions in their wake. The story is progressing with smart plot twists, both in actions and in emotions. If this reader has one regret while reading this series, it would be that this entry is only book two in a proposed six book series. The next cannot come soon enough.—Stacey Hayman

_____. **Lies**. *A Gone Novel.* Katherine Tegen, 2010. 464p. $17.99. 978-0-06-144909-3. $9.99 Trade pb. 978-0-06-144911-6.
VOYA June 2010. **5Q · 5P · J · S** (SF/F/H)
Teens' Top Ten 2011.

It's been four months since everyone over fifteen disappeared from the FAYZ and those who have survived the strange changes are continuing to adapt. Some community infrastructures, like food collection and distribution, currency, and a town council, have been established but remain weak, and they are about to get weaker. Caine needs to sneak through town so he can steal a boat and get his remaining followers to an island mansion they believe has food. To provide a distraction, Caine arms the Human Crew with guns and gasoline leading to maximum destruction. But most troublesome of all could be the visions Orsay is having of the outside world. Are they real? Is she right to encourage kids turning fifteen to take the poof, saying they will be reunited with their families? Or are they actually committing suicide, or worse, as Astrid strongly believes.

This book retains all the great action, unexpected twists, and engaging characters of the previous stories; readers will learn the answers to old questions but new questions continue to proliferate. As the series has progressed, the intensity of the stories has also been progressing. Descriptions of the violence are more graphic, discussions of good vs. evil are deeper, and the kids are indulging more often in adult activities, like drinking and taking drugs. Fascinating, frightening, and absolutely worth an obsessive wait for the next installment, mature teen readers will embrace this thrill ride tempered with a touch of smart social commentary.—Stacey Hayman.

Green, John. **The Fault in Our Stars**. Dutton/Penguin, 2012. 336p. $17.99. 978-0-525-47881-2.
VOYA April 2012. **5Q · 5P · S**
YALSA Readers' Choice List 2013

Hazel Grace is a sixteen-year-old cancer patient, caught up in the effort it takes to live in a body that everyone knows is running out of time. When she reluctantly agrees to return to her local teen cancer support group to satisfy her mother, the last thing she expects is an encounter with destiny. New to the group, Augustus Waters is handsome, bitingly sarcastic, and in remission. He is also immediately taken with Hazel, and what begins as a casual friendship soon escalates into a full romance. Through an impressive exchange of books and words, philosophies and metaphors, Hazel and Augustus tear apart what it means to be both star-crossed lovers and imminently mortal.

Green's much-anticipated novel is breathtaking in its ability to alternate between iridescent humor and raw tragedy. Hazel and Augustus are both fully realized, complex characters that each defy what it means to be a cancer patient in a unique way. While Hazel fixates about how her death will eventually hurt her loved ones, Augustus obsesses about how he will be remembered; the two are drawn together by the justified anxiety they feel over endings. If **The Fault in Our Stars** has a fault, it is not that Green's writing is too complex for teens, as some suggest, but that at times the complexity of Green's voice overshadows the narrative. Purchase for small and large libraries alike, though several copies may be wise considering both Green's popularity, and the potential of this book to become a classic.—Allison Hunter Hill.

Green, Simon R. **The Unnatural Inquirer**. *Nightside*. Ace Books, 2008. 246p. $7.99 pb. 978-0-441-01667-9.
VOYA June 2008. **5Q · 5P · S · A/YA** (SF/F/H)

Any book where the heroically gruff private detective must run between the legs of a caged Tyrannosaurus Rex is obviously worth a peek, and this one more than lives up to that moment. Infamous John Taylor, a PI renowned for his exploits in a supernatural underworld known as the Nightside, is hired by resident scandal rag The Unnatural Inquirer to track down and get to the bottom of an apparent recording of the Afterlife. Despite the fact that John already has a tortured romance with a famed Nightside bounty hunter, he partners up with a beautiful tabloid reporter to get to the truth and stay ahead of the more powerful players in the Nightside. Populated with bizarre supporting characters, including resident authority Walker, the church token-stealing Cardinal, and the chilling Removal Man, the Nightside is a clever blend of gritty detective story and SF comedy, although Green goes more for grit than laughs in most cases.

Reading the previous seven books, beginning with **Something from the Nightside** (Ace Books, 2003), is not necessary, even though readers are dropped in the middle of Taylor's adventures. Discussion of past cases plays more as a demonstration of his celebrity than as something missed. The language is a little coarse and violence is prevalent, but they fit the story and the types of tales to which it pays tribute in its own special way. Get past the goblins and squint a little, and a story worthy of Dashiell Hammett or Raymond Chandler will emerge.—Matthew Weaver.

Griffin, Paul. **Burning Blue**. Dial/Penguin, 2012. 288p. $17.99. 978-0-8037-3815-7.
VOYA August 2012. **5Q · 5P · J · S**

Nicole Castro had beauty, a rich family, and popularity. That was until acid was thrown onto her face and she was permanently disfigured. As Nicole tries to recover and adjust to her life with half of her face bandaged and scarred, she is plagued by news crews trying to follow her story, her fear of being seen, and constant pain. She also fears that her attacker will strike again. But who was cruel enough to do such a thing to Nicole? Even though Jay is not friends with Nicole before the accident, as he decides to search for the perpetrator, he finds himself growing closer to her.

Burning Blue has all of the elements of classic mystery writing: a criminal act, numerous suspects with motive, and red herrings. The modern setting and situations will make this mystery a hit with young adults. The characters are believable, well-developed, and flawed. Jay, the computer-hacking outsider, throws himself into a unique mystery-solving journey and discovers startling evidence that makes one wonder how far a person will go to get what they want. A dull moment does not exist in this fast-paced, modern mystery. This book will be a great addition to any fiction collection for adolescents.—Dianna Geers.

_____. **The Orange Houses**. Dial, 2009. 147p. $16.99. 978-0-8037-3346-6. $7.99 Trade pb. 978-0-14-241982-3.
VOYA October 2009. **5Q · 5P · J · S**
Top Ten Best Books for Young Adults 2010.

Jimmi Sixes, an eighteen-year-old Iraq war veteran, is about to be hanged. He has rescued fifteen-year-old Tamika, who should stop bleeding from serious cuts, but Fatima is still in big trouble. All this action happens before page one. Is it reasonable to expect readers to keep turning the page? Absolutely. These teens inhabit the ugly underbelly of the Bronx where poverty, ignorance, and violence threaten to derail their determination to succeed. Jimmi, a drug addicted poet, is Tamika's (Mik) protector. Mik, tormented because of her hearing aids, turns them off to enjoy the quiet while pursuing her drawing. Fatima, tall, beautiful, serene, and persistently optimistic, is an illegal alien who fled an unnamed African country after a savage attack that left her tragically maimed. She teaches paper folding at the local VA and is saving to bring family members to America, while staying under the radar.

The chapter headings never let the reader forget that something awful is going to happen by the end of the book—"twenty-seven days before the hanging"; "eighteen days before the hanging"; "Twenty-four minutes before the hanging"—but Griffin lures his audience with authentic dialogue, an uncompromising take on the harsh realities of ghetto life, and his characters' heroic determination to save, if not themselves, then at least each other. A rich smorgasbord of themes demands provocative classroom discussion about bullying, war, illegal immigration, and last but so not least, friendship.—Beth E. Andersen.

Grimes, Nikki. **Bronx Masquerade**. Dial, 2002. 176p. $16.99. 0-8037-2569-8. $6.99 pb. 978-0-14-250189-4.
VOYA February 2002. **5Q · 5P · J · S**
Coretta Scott King Award 2003.
Best Books for Young Adults 2003.
Quick Picks for Reluctant Young Adult Readers 2003.
Popular Paperbacks for Young Adults 2007.

Mr. Ward's English class is unlike any his students have experienced before. In his inner city Bronx, New York, high school classroom, Mr. Ward takes his eighteen students into the personal, heartfelt world of writing poetry during their study of the Harlem Renaissance. Each chapter is told by a different teen, allowing readers insight into the teens' feelings about themselves and their classmates through beautifully crafted poems that they share on Open Mike Fridays. Devon Hope writes, "Maybe it's time I just started being who I am." This honest admission is just one of many that the characters make.

What begins with eighteen disjointed people becomes a newfound family, united in compassion and camaraderie against a backdrop of broken homes, peer pressure, and tumultuous relationships. Readers will become immersed in the lives of these students with their natural teen-speak: "And guess what? That white boy can flow. Makes you kinda wonder 'bout his family tree, now don't it?" Grimes addresses many of today's teen issues through the characters' unforgettable voices and poems. In the spirit of Gil Alicea's memoir **The Air Down Here** (Chronicle, 1995), this book will be an exciting addition to urban public and school libraries and will serve well in teen poetry classes, speaking to the poet in every teen who picks it up.—Beth Gilbert.

Hainsworth, Emily. **Through to You**. Balzer + Bray/HarperCollins, 2012. 272p. $17.99. 978-0-06-209419-3.
VOYA June 2012. **5Q · 5P · J · S**

Camden Pike lost everything the night his girlfriend, Viv, died in a tragic accident. She kept him sane when his career as a football star ended, when his father abandoned the family, and when his workaholic mother coped by being more absent. Now all he has is his memories and Viv's shrine to comfort him. While visiting the site of the deadly crash, an eerie green light appears, and there is a girl named Nina on the other side calling to him. Although he does not recognize the girl, he soon learns that the green light is a portal into a parallel world where Viv is still alive. Determined to have her back, Camden ignores Nina's warnings about the other Viv and seeks to make his life whole again. As the portal begins shrinking, Camden finds himself at the center of dangerous secrets and deadly obsessions.

Hainsworth's debut novel is fresh, exciting, and haunting. Through her portrayal of a grieving young man, she explores the question that plagues so many in real life: "What if?" Although the novel is classified as a sci-fi thriller, it deals with real themes and real issues that face people of all ages (i.e., grief, trust, relationships, and identity). The well-developed characters help readers make an immediate emotional connection that results in a personal investment in the outcome of the story. Although there is a moderate amount of foul language sprinkled throughout the novel, it is a must-have for any classroom or library shelf.—Courtney M. Krieger.

Hale, Shannon. **Princess Academy: Palace of Stone**. Bloomsbury, 2012. 336p. $16.99. 978-1-599-90873-1.
VOYA October 2012. **5Q · 5P · M · J · S · A/YA**

This sequel to the bestselling **Princess Academy** (Bloomsbury, 2005/VOYA August 2005) picks up where the 2006 Newbery Honor book left off, with Miri and her friends coming down from their isolated quarry village on Mount Eskel to a new life in the capital city, Asland. There, the resilient heroine, Miri, assists the future princess, Britta (who won the hand of the prince in the first book), prepare for the royal wedding while having the opportunity to continue her education at the queen's Castle. Miri enjoys making new friends and experiencing life in an exciting, unfamiliar environment, although she soon realizes political intrigue permeates the lowland city, and the personal strengths she discovered at the Princess Academy will again be put to careful use.

Hale has written a worthy and complex continuation of Miri's story, and her strong and vibrant character will be familiar and welcome to readers of the first book, despite the length between publications. A literary and engaging coming-of-age story, the elements of class tension, home, family, friendship, and self discovery ring true. Likely to be included on many notable books lists for 2012, this is an essential purchase for school and public libraries.—Elaine Gass Hirsch.

Harder, Jens. **Leviathan**. ComicsLit/NBM, 2004, ©2003. 144p. 978-2-84856-015-1. O.P.
VOYA December 2004. **5Q · 5P · J · S · A/YA** (SF/F/H)

Quelle astonishment! This selection is less a graphic novel than it is an experience: They do not make them like it anymore-if they ever did. Presenting a wordless epic but for the whale-related quotes in four languages from the Bible, philosophers, and Moby Dick, Harder offers astonishing pictorials and stories wide open for interpretation. A ship full of missionaries alights on an island, only to discover that it is far more dangerous than they would think. One of the leviathans in question leaves a trail of nautical wreckage in its path, including the gods, Ahab's *Pequod*, the *Titanic*, and *Noah's Ark*, while another (or the same one?) dukes it out with a giant squid.

Perhaps in part because of its original French 2003 release, the book plays like a foreign silent film, in which the words are not important and from which one never wants to tear away one's eyes. Teen readers, especially those with their own thoughts of dabbling in drawing, fantasy, or simply bizarre stream-of-consciousness, should enjoy the opportunity to forge their own ideas of the action within. This imagining of the whale in life and personality is an incredible concept made even more unbelievable by the beauty and complexity of the artwork. It is a virtual visual buffet, and Harder's readers are helpless to do anything but grab on to the whale by the tail, hang on, and enjoy the ride.—Matthew Weaver.

Harrington, Hannah. **Saving June**. Harlequin Teen, 2011. 376p. $18.99. 978-0-373-21024-4.

VOYA June 2011. **5Q · 5P · S · A/YA**

Harper Scott's older sister, June, commits suicide two weeks shy of her high school graduation. So Harper, at sixteen, defiantly finds herself an only child while mourning her sister's death and is not kind to her divorced and grief-stricken parents. To make matters worse, Harper is the one who finds her deceased sister. But a huge unanswered question for Harper is why? June does not even leave behind a goodbye note. Meanwhile, Tyler hangs around during the wake at Harper's house. Harper ponders his connection to her late sister and investigates clues regarding June's unfulfilled dreams. This takes her on a road trip to California with her best friend, Laney, and Tyler to scatter her sister's ashes into the Pacific Ocean. Along the way, they encounter adventure among their far-flung friends and acquaintances. Just when you discover Tyler's connection to Harper's sister, the climax takes the reader on a gigantic twist.

This is a work of realistic fiction. The author portrays the life of wayward teens who seek independence. Although the language may be a bit salty, it is realistic. The story also includes the theme of budding romance, with some sexual expression. Saving June should become a movie some day—it even includes a soundtrack.—Sharon Blumberg.

Hautman, Pete. **All-In**. Simon & Schuster, 2007. 192p. $16.99. 978-1-4169-1325-2. $5.99 pb. 978-1-4169-1326-9.

VOYA June 2007. **5Q · 5P · J · S**

This novel picks up where Hautman's **No Limit** (originally published as **Stone Cold**, Simon & Schuster, 1998/**VOYA** February 1999) leaves off. In that book, fifteen-year-old Denn Doyle discovers that he possesses such a gift for playing poker that by the end of the story, he has won a restaurant, enraging its former owner, professional gambler Artie Kingston. This sequel opens with Denn, now seventeen, living in Vegas, playing serious, serious poker for serious, serious stakes-the kind of scary money that one sees played on cable television. Denn is on an unbeatable streak-he is a master at studying "tells," the oh-so-subtle body language, facial expressions, and gambling behaviors of his opponents that Denn uses to decipher their hands and spot their bluffs. But Denn's luck flips dramatically. Kingston is in Vegas, obsessed with destroying Denn by using Denn's new girlfriend, the deeply damaged Cattie Hart, a casino card handler with lightning hands, to seal the deal. Denn is quickly ruined, stunned that his downward spiral was precipitated by Cattie's treachery. Kingston is not done with Denn. He sets up a winner-take-all, million-dollar game, knowing that Denn cannot resist. Denn works his way back just far enough to meet the minimum ante, and the tension cranks up to unbearable levels as Denn and Artie go after each other, poker hand by poker hand.

Skillfully using the multiple-voice approach, Hautman brings to life the intricacies of poker, crafting a thrilling story of loss, good versus evil, and redemption. Best read after one finishes **No Limit**, Hautman's story is of such appealing excitement that it is guaranteed to make parents and teachers uneasy.—Beth E. Andersen.

_____. **Invisible**. Simon & Schuster, 2005. 160p. $16.99. 978-0-689-86800-9. $7.99 Trade pb. 978-0-689-86903-7.
VOYA August 2005. **5Q · 5P · M · J · S**
Best Books for Young Adults 2006.

Doug Hanson is as profoundly disturbed as a teen can get. At seventeen, he still communicates with his best friend, Andy, killed two years ago in a fire that Doug was partly responsible for setting. Targeted in high school by his fellow students for his deeply weird behavior, Doug loses himself in the basement of his home, constructing an exquisitely detailed miniature railroad, complete with bridges and people and town buildings, all made out of headless matchsticks. Doug's home life is a misery. His bullying, punishing, professor father has cowed Doug's mother and will not tolerate Doug's obvious slide toward a mental breakdown, despite regular sessions with a therapist. Mr. Hanson cannot tolerate imperfection even when Doug is caught stalking a fellow student and the police come knocking.

With excruciating care, Hautman builds an unbearable tension toward disaster. At the beginning of the book, Doug has designed a sigil, a seal using a combination of Doug's and Andy's initials. As the story careens toward inevitable tragedy, the sigil devolves into ever more obscure versions until it is an unreadable but arresting sign of impending horror. Schools and parents continue to ignore the costs of bullying at their own and their children's peril. Hautman takes the reader into the very core of the victim and the dynamics of heartless targeting, and forces all to accept responsibility for stopping the cycle of violence.—Beth E. Andersen.

Hawkins, Rachel. **Demonglass**. *Hex Hall*. Disney Hyperion, 2011. 368p. $16.99. 978-1-4231-2131-2.
VOYA December 2010. **5Q · 5P · M · J · S** (SF/F/H)
Teens' Top Ten 2011.

Last year, Sophie Mercer was sent to Hecate Hall, a place for troubled and troublesome young Prodigium (or magical beings), in hopes that she could get control of her powers before someone got hurt, including herself. Hex Hall also turned out to be the place where the L'Occhio di Dio, aka The Eye, was literally able to take a stab at killing her. Summer vacation is going to be different. Sophie is headed for England where she is going to be living under the protective guardianship of the Prodigium's Head of the Council, a gentleman who happens to be a powerful demon and who also happens to be the father she had never met. Bringing her best friend, Jenna, and her betrothed, Cal, Sophie is feeling optimistic about getting to know her dad, learning how to use her powers, and maybe running into her forbidden crush, Archer Cross, fellow Hex Hall student and perpetrator of the attempted stabbing. Or maybe a complicated and dangerous situation is about to spiral out of control?

Sophie's well-crafted banter, her conflicted feelings over the two stellar boys claiming her attention, and her struggles to understand the history, politics, and social maneuvering of the magical world, merge into one engaging, entertaining story. Once readers turn the first page, it is nearly impossible to put the book down because they will be looking for the next "swoony" feeling or because they will be desperate to know what happens next or because it just cannot end that way. This reader is now firmly planted on the edge of her seat, waiting for the third *Hex Hall* book.—Stacey Hayman.

Herbsman, Cheryl Renée. **Breathing**. Viking, 2009. 272p. $16.99. 978-0-670-01123-0. $7.99 pb. 978-0-14-241601-3.
   VOYA October 2009. **5Q · 5P · M · J · S · A/YA**
   Named for a tornado that was devastating Georgia at the time of her birth, Savannah Georgina Brown is a charming, conflicted character. Growing up in a small coastal town in North Carolina, Savannah has always known that someday she would fly the coop and discover bigger and better things in the world. The summer she turns fifteen and a half, however, Savannah contemplates throwing away all her chances to leave town. The cause of her dramatic change of heart is eighteen-year-old Jackson Channing, who has arrived in town to stay with relatives. The entire tragedy and uncertainty of his young life grabs hold of Savannah the first time they meet. From the start, the two are inseparable, literally saving each other's' lives twice. But when Jackson is called home, Savannah starts to panic: how will she be able to breathe without him?
   With a narrative voice that feels as comfortable and authentic as Judy Blume's yet captures the regional dialect of the Southeast, Herbsman perfectly nails the angst, innocence, and beauty of falling in love for the first time. The creative use of Savannah's life-threatening asthma as a symbol of her dependence on others is not heavy handed and is utterly believable. This book is sure to reach teen readers in a way that few books can: as she embarks on a summer of passion and discovery, Savannah might just be the girl next door . . . or the girl in the mirror. —Jennifer McConnel.

Hiaasen, Carl. **Scat**. Knopf, 2009. 384p. $16.99. 978-0-375-83486-8. PLB $19.99. 978-0-375-93486-5. $8.99 Trade pb. 978-0-375-83487-5.
   VOYA April 2009. **5Q · 5P · M · J**
   Hiassen makes an effortless transition from adult to young adult novels with his ingeniously engineered and popular eco-mysteries set in the swamps of Florida. This latest book is no exception. The hero is a seemingly ordinary middle school boy named Nick. The mystery begins when Nick's biology teacher, Mrs. Starch, a notorious curmudgeon reminiscent of Viola Swamp of **The Teacher from the Black Lagoon** (Scholastic, 1989), shepherds Nick's class on a field trip to the Everglades. When the students are evacuated because of a fire in the swamp, Mrs. Starch suddenly vanishes. Nick and his friend Marta decide to investigate. Along with the mystery of Mrs. Starch's disappearance, there are other strange events that puzzle Nick and Marta. Of course, these mysteries are connected somehow, and that is what makes the story so enjoyable. But the light and humorous plot is tempered by more serious concerns. Nick's father, a soldier serving in Iraq, has lost his arm in a roadside explosion and has returned home to recuperate. There are also the bumbling but dastardly villains who have devised a scheme to make money at the expense of the environment. As the reader expects, Nick manages to neatly solve the mystery and avert ecological catastrophe. Nick's resilience is quite remarkable, making him an appealing if perhaps a tad unrealistic hero.

The many subplots to this complex mystery, however, are skillfully intertwined. Several characters also delight the reader by revealing unexpected sides to their personalities. This book will undoubtedly be a big hit with fans of Hiassen's other novels, **Flush** (Knopf, 2005/**VOYA** October 2005) and **Hoot** (Knopf, 2002/**VOYA** October 2002).—Jan Chapman.

High, Linda Oatman. **Planet Pregnancy**. Front Street/Boyds Mills, 2009, ©2008. 197p. $11.95 Trade pb. 978-1-59078-767-0.
   VOYA June 2009. **5Q · 5P · J · S**
   Quick Picks for Reluctant Young Readers 2009.
   Seventeen-year-old Sahara has just left Texas and entered Planet Pregnancy, inhabited only by herself and "Embryo." Sahara cannot imagine how she could be pregnant because "tragedy happens to other people, not me." When Sahara becomes the stereotypical "catastrophe," she is understandably frightened and shies from revealing her circumstances to those who might provide help and support as she attempts to make a decision that will alter the rest of her life. As the days tick by and Sahara remains silent, she is overwhelmed by the only three options she can conceive: to become a young mother, to give up her child for adoption, or to "Take Care Of It" and try to move beyond her mistake. Alone with her thoughts, Sahara's terror deepens as her condition progresses, and her options quickly begin to run out.
   Told in free verse that lends authenticity to the narrator's teen voice, this novel chronicles the momentous nine-month journey that Sahara enters, starting with the shocking results of her home pregnancy test and ending after the delivery of her child. The discomforts of pregnancy and the anguish of being seventeen and on the verge of adult life are presented with humor and honesty, making Sahara leap off the page and become a girl who could be found in any school, anywhere in modern America. Although some readers might disagree with Sahara's ultimate choice, the novel is a realistic and compelling read for any teen.—Jennifer McConnel.

Hoeye, Michael. **Sands of Time**. *A Hermux Tantamoq Adventure*. G. P. Putnam's Sons/Penguin Putnam, 2002. 277p. $15. 978-1-4223-5951-8.
   VOYA December 2002. **5Q · 5P · M · J** (SF/F/H)
   Hermux Tantamoq, watchmaker and gentle mouse-about-town, is back in this second adventure of amateur sleuthing. Intrigue abounds following the "cat"astrophic opening of the new exhibit at the Pinchester Museum of Art and Science. Mirrin Stentrill's visionary paintings of the mystical CAT Kingdom have the militant rodent population all a-twitter. Cats have long been taboo, and Mayor Hooster Pinkwiggin vows to shut the exhibit down. Complications arise when Mirrin's beloved chipmunk fiancé, Birch Tentintrotter, long presumed dead, reappears with an ancient map leading to the lost kingdom of cats. Will Hermux, Birch, and the plucky, yet bored aviatrix, Linka Perflinger, find the ancient tomb of Ka Narsh-Pa and unlock the hidden secrets of CATS? Will the self-serving cosmetics tycoon, Tucka Mertslin, claim the hidden cat treasures for herself? Will revisionist historian Hickum Stepfitcher III rewrite mouse history for

another generation? The race is on and the adventure begins. Can a cat be in love with a mouse? Did cats ever really exist? Will Hermux finally find his love reciprocated?

The crackling, witty dialogue of **Time Stops for No Mouse** (Putnam's, 2002/**VOYA** June 2002) continues in this second *Hermux Tantamoq Adventure*. The crisp sense of time and place again paints a full picture of the multi-specied citizens of Pinchester. Alive with humor, dastardly deeds, courage, and honor, this novel will have readers nibbling at the bit for the next installment of the adventures of Hermux Tantamoq.—Marian Rafal.

Hopkins, Ellen. **Fallout**. Simon & Schuster, 2010. 672p. $18.99. 978-1-4169-5009-7.
VOYA October 2010. **5Q · 5P · S · A/YA**

Hopkins uses free form verse and alternates the stories of three of Kristina Snow's teen-age offspring to show the effects of her meth addiction on their lives. Adopted by Kristina's mother, Hunter Haskins lives in Reno and does not know his father. With his angry outbursts, heavy drinking, and cheating, Hunter imperils his serious relationship with girlfriend Nikki. Seventeen-year-old Autumn Shepherd doesn't remember her mother and, with her father, Trey, in prison, she lives in San Antonio with his sister. Autumn suffers from panic attacks and obsessive-compulsion disorder (OCD), and uses alcohol to ease her pain. Summer Kenwood, now fifteen, has been "drop kicked around" placement homes and endured sexual abuse. When her father, Ron, gets picked up for drunken driving, Summer lands in foster care again but runs away with sexy meth-using Kyle. Circumstances throw all three together at Christmas. They confront, not only their mother, but the jarring reality of the choices they are making.

Containing f-bombs and some sexual description, Hopkins' pithy poetry is the perfect vehicle to deliver the festering emotional beating that drug addiction inflicts on families. The experience is painful enough suffered vicariously and might jostle readers into examining their own decisions about drugs and alcohol. Unfortunately, many will find themselves in similar circumstances through no fault of their own. In the "Author's Note," Hopkins offers them understanding and direction for "breaking the cycle." A quick read considering its page length, Fallout is impossible to put down. Last in the trilogy (**Crank**, **Glass**), it is also a powerful stand-alone.—Barbara Johnston.

_____. **Perfect**. Margaret K. McElderry/Simon & Schuster, 2011. 640p. $18.99. 978-1-4169-8324-8.
VOYA October 2011. **5Q · 5P · S**
Quick Picks for Reluctant Young Readers 2012.

A companion to **Impulse** (Simon & Schuster, 2007/VOYA February 2007), this vigorous verse novel highlights Conner's twin sister, Cara; her sporty boyfriend, Sean; pageant queen and model Kendra; and rich, aspiring dancer Andre. At its nucleus, four teenagers are grappling with insecurities that become exacerbated when loved ones turn up the heat. Cara's brother has attempted suicide, spotlighting an inexpressive mother who stresses distinction rather than showing affection. Similarly, Kendra's mother turns a blind eye to her daughter's anorexia, while Andre's parents' expectations keep him from pursuing his dance dream, and Sean's father's fixation with his baseball prowess fuels Sean's steroid abuse. Within these dilemmas, two begin to blossom while two begin to seethe.

The unrestricted access Hopkins employs is formidable: parents, siblings, love interests, and outliers all thrust frank judgment on the characters. It is how Cara, Sean, Kendra, and Andre react that encourages readers' emotional attachments. Her writing conveys teenage quandaries with all of the intended consequences, as the verse style only serves to shock as the events unfold. The ill-fated conclusion continues to establish Hopkins as a realist, someone with vested concern for the challenges teens face daily from cyberbullying, dating violence, sexual orientation, prejudice, and fractured families. Ideally, readers will want to read Impulse first, as events began there and conclude here, but those who invest in Perfect will also be looking to find out the fate of these characters in the near future.—Alicia Abdul.

Horowitz, Anthony. **The Devil and His Boy**. Philomel, 2000. 182p. PLB $15.99. 978-1-4395-1669-0. $6.99 pb. 978-0-14-240797-4.
VOYA April 2000. **5Q · 5P · M · J**

Tom Falconer, a thirteen-year-old orphan living in the sixteenth century, is grossly underfed and overworked by evil innkeepers Sebastian and Henrietta Slope. He is unaware of the adventures in store for him. In the span of just a few short days, he is rescued by a knight, pursued on horseback by famed highwayman Gamaliel Ratsey, nearly mutilated by the leader of a gang of beggars, introduced to William Shakespeare, hired by an acting troupe, and he performs before Queen Elizabeth and saves the entire English monarchy-all without a clue about what is happening to him or what he should do next. This is the story of a true innocent, struggling to survive in a world of villainy, poverty, tyranny, duplicity, deceit, and subterfuge.

In this delightful and inventive mixture of historical fact and grand storytelling, Horowitz has conjured a fabulous, fast-paced tale of humor, intrigue, magic, and adventure that any young adult will find satisfying. The characters are especially vivid-full of rotten teeth, scarred faces, moldy dispositions, and almost all based on actual people. Gone, but not missed, is the love interest that can often bog down an otherwise swiftly moving story line. Neither does one miss the high-handed moralizing that usually surrounds the introduction of disreputable characters like highwaymen or pickpockets. No, there is not a moral lesson, just a great fun read. And isn't it about time for one of those? If you booktalk this highly recommended purchase for all public, private, and school libraries, you will need multiple copies.—Dr. Stefani Koorey.

Hubbard, Mandy. **You Wish**. Razorbill, 2010. 284p. $8.99 Trade pb. 978-1-59514-292-4.
VOYA October 2010. **5Q · 5P · J · S**

Sixteen-year-old Kayla McHenry must be dreaming. There is no way a prancing, living, breathing, pink My Pretty Pony can be following her around—no way all her wishes up to her sixteenth birthday are suddenly coming true. Kayla is an intelligent, but cynical and sarcastic, teen who put all of these childish dreams behind her. But remaining cool and aloof proves harder than she planned when she finds Ann in her closet, full-sized and ready to play. Mandy Hubbard does a remarkable job of capturing the spirit of a sullen teen who wants nothing more than to mock the popular kids at school.

This coming-of-age book will appeal to young adult readers with its humor, likeable characters, and smooth reading style. Kayla, her best friend, Nicole, and Nicole's boyfriend, Ben, are in a tangled triangle of friendship, loyalty, and honesty, where everything is tested. Readers will eagerly tag along with Kayla as she discovers that who she is may not be who she wants to be. And while she may have outgrown things from her childhood, she may just learn it's not childish to want what you had when you were young. Readers will love this fantastically funny, heart-warming book about getting much more than you wish for.—Juli Zimmerman.

Issues in the Digital Age. Reference Point, 2011. 96p. PLB $27.95. Further Reading. Websites.
VOYA April 2012. **5Q · 5P · M · J · S · A/YA** (NF)
Currie, Stephen. **Online Privacy**. 978-1-60152-194-1.
Mooney, Carla. **Online Security**. 978-1-60152-195-8.

Issues in the Digital Age is a very informative series. Two of the books from this series, Online Security and Online Privacy are such important topics in today's world of technology that it is wonderful to see easy-to-understand information available for adults and teens alike. Safety and privacy in regards to technology can be overwhelming topics for the average consumer; fortunately, this series does a very good job of breaking these topics down into manageable chunks within each chapter. The "Facts About…" section at the end of each book is very interesting and would be a good addition in reports or presentations. The "Related Organizations" section is provides very helpful information for further research.

This is a wonderful series for any classroom teacher having students research technology in the world today. It would be especially helpful in technology education classes where learning to navigate the computer and become computer savvy are important topics. Counselors and administrators would find these books helpful when presenting parent workshops on technology and how to help their children—and themselves—use it safely. This series would be an excellent addition both in the media center as well as the classroom, or guidance office.—Lona Trulove.

Jacques, Brian. **The Legend of Luke**. *A Tale of Redwall*. Philomel, 2000. 384p. $23.95. 978-0-399-23490-3. $7.99 pb. 978-0-441-00773-8.
VOYA April 2000. **5Q · 5P · M · J** (SF/F/H)

As Trimp, a hedgehog from the cold northland coast, gazes upon the beauty of Mossflower Country and observes the pride and friendliness of the animals building Redwall Abbey, she is overwhelmed. After a scrumptious Redwall lunch, Trimp volunteers to help Martin the Warrior, founder of Redwall, hoist a roof beam. To lift the spirits of the animals as well, Trimp sings a song about Martin's father, Luke the Warrior. The song awakens memories in Martin, creating a desire to see where he was born as well as to discover if his father has returned to the northland shore as promised. Recognizing Martin's self-sacrifice and acknowledging all he has done for them, the other animals pack provisions for his journey. With Trimp and two trusted comrades, Martin begins his quest filled with hair-raising, swashbuckling adventures. Readers are also treated to the magnificent, spellbinding exploits of Luke the Warrior, including his relentless pursuit of Vilu Daskar, the pirate stoat responsible for the murder of his wife, Martin's mother.

As in the eleven previous *Redwall* sagas, this tale abounds with fast-paced adventure, courage, hardship, love, unwavering loyalty, dastardly villains, admirable heroes, cowards, humor, and friendships that enrapture and mesmerize the reader. Jacques again has created a magical tale filled with nonstop action and unforgettable characters. Although this volume fills in gaps and adds to the lore of *Redwall*, newcomers to the series will not be disappointed. For *Redwall* enthusiasts, it is an absolute must!-Bill Mollineaux.

_____. **Sable Quean**. *A Tale of Redwall*. Philomel, 2010. 416p. $23.99. 978-0-399-25164-1. $7.99 pb. 978-0-441-01998-4.
VOYA December 2009. **5Q · 5P · M · J** (SF/F/H)

This latest *Redwall* title makes the case that Jacques's twenty-one volume series is among the top tier of consistently excellent storytelling. Just turned seventy, the master shows no signs of letting up or slowing down the action of his sweeping sagas that play out in the lives of the gentle critters of Mossflower Wood. In classic Jacquesian style, several story threads fire up quickly, effectively snaring any beast meandering about the first several pages. With his loyal sidekick Diggs, the heroic and rebellious Buckler, Blademaster hare of the Long Patrol, sets out from Salamandastron on a journey to Redwall Abbey. Meanwhile fiendish Zwilt the Shade orchestrates an insidious plan to take over the Abbey with his band of vermin, the Ravagers. Even more ruthless is Zwilt's commander, Vilaya the evil Sable Quean.

Predictable? Yes. Formulaic? Of course. No matter. *Redwall* addicts do not feverishly hunt down Jacques's titles because they expect the unexpected. What might be drawbacks in the hands of a less-experienced descriptor become solid and familiar foundations upon which Jacques weaves fantastic adventure and swashbuckling action embellished with delicious detail. The tale of Buckler, Zwilt the Shade, and Vilaya runs to a satisfying end leaving fans counting the days until the next series title, but it can be picked up anywhere. This installment is just as good a starting point as any of the previous twenty titles. Tweens and young teens will line up for it, and multiple copies will not go unread. No doubt freshly infected hordes will want to snap up as many previous titles as they can lay their hands on. —Lauri J. Vaughan.

_____. **Triss**. *A Tale of Redwall*. Philomel, 2002. 432p. $23.99. 978-0-399-23723-2. $7.99 pb. 978-0-441-01095-0.
VOYA December 2002. **5Q · 5P · M · J · S** (SF/F/H)

Fervent *Redwall* fans and newcomers will welcome the fifteenth book in this highly acclaimed and popular series. Scrumptious feasts, rollicking humor, swashbuckling heroes, faithful friends, and treacherous villains magically combine through three intertwined action-packed plots into one unforgettable, spellbinding story. When two Dibbuns, tired of going to bed early, sneak off into the Mossflower woodland and get lost, they accidentally discover the forgotten secret entrance to Brockhall, the original home of the badgers, but they are unable to remember the exact location. Triss, a brave squirrelmaid slave, escapes the clutches of the evil ferret King Agarnu and his murderous daughter Princess Kurda, incurring Kurda's wrath and unquenchable thirst for revenge. After capturing the newly built ship that was to take Kurda and her bumbling brother Prince Bladd to Mossflower to find out if the previous king is alive or dead, Agarnu hires treacherous freebooters to carry out the mission, enabling vengeful Kurda to pursue Triss. The rebellious son of the great badger ruler of Salamandastron and his friend run away, searching for adventure and wind up joining forces with Triss and the Redwallers as they discover Brockhall and defeat the freebooters. Jacques combines these three stories with three smelly and sinister snakes and a secret code that is the key to discovering Brockhall's location, rewarding readers with an unforgettable adventure.

Readers will want to use the code to decipher and reply to the invitation at the story's conclusion. When animal fantasy buffs have sated themselves with all the *Redwall* books, they might enjoy Avi's *Poppy* series, Robin Jarvis's *Deptford Mice* trilogy, and books by David Clement-Davies.—Bill Mollineaux.

James, Rebecca. **Beautiful Malice**. Random House, 2010. 272p. $25. 978-0-553-80805-6.

VOYA August 2010. **5Q · 5P · J · S**

Katherine Patterson used to be someone else—Katie Boydell, a popular high school junior and loving older sister to Rachel. After Rachel is brutally murdered, public speculation grows into a vicious condemnation of the family and slowly kills Katie too. Adopting her mother's maiden name, attending a new high school, and blending into the background, Katherine is going through the motions until she meets the charismatic Alice. Drawn into Alice's world of extremes, Katherine feels alive again, even when Alice's behavior is inappropriate, or even cruel. Robbie, victim of unrequited love for Alice, shares Katherine's reluctance to leave behind such obvious trouble, even after witnessing multiple examples of her questionable morals. An unexpected chain of events leads Katherine back to a safer, healthier path, with the potential for a true best friend and perhaps even the love of her life. But will Katherine be able to leave Alice and her past behind?

There are three complete, complex story lines intricately woven to form a delicate balance between the story telling the events of the present, the distant past, and a more recent past. Each portion builds upon the others, and they all become progressively more suspenseful, more dramatic, and more terrific. Clues from the past are slowly revealed and help build tension until the end. With such engaging characters, you'll want an untainted happy ending, but you'll get something even better: a satisfying end. This debut novel will grab your attention on the first page, and you won't want to turn away even after the last page has been turned.—Stacey Hayman.

Jinks, Catherine. **Pagan in Exile**. *Pagan Chronicles*. Candlewick, 2004. 336p. $15.99. 978-0-7636-2020-2. $6.99 pb. 978-0-7636-2691-4.
VOYA April 2004. **5Q · 5P · M · J**

This second book in Jinks's four-part series about Pagan Kidrouk, squire to Lord Roland Roucy de Bram of the Knights Templar, is every bit as good as her first book, **Pagan's Crusade** (Candlewick, 2003/**VOYA** December 2003). The year is 1188, and having fought for and lost Jerusalem to Muslim forces, seventeen-year-old Pagan, a Christian Arab, accompanies Roland to the latter's native France. There Roland presses his powerful father to join Pope Gregory's Crusade to retake the Holy Land. Fat chance. "The Pope can eat stewed scorpions and die," says Roland's father. He is preoccupied, locked in a power struggle with the nearby Abbey, and wisely loathe to entrust the family lands to the tender mercies of Roland's unlovely, squabbling older brothers. Inevitably, Pagan and Roland are drawn into the local secular versus religious brawl-high-minded and naïve Roland as would-be peacemaker and Pagan, the wise-cracking, former Jerusalem street urchin, as a savvy but ever more horrified observer concerned for his master's safety. In the process and in dialogue with each other, both Pagan and Roland come to question their most basic assumptions about the world and themselves.

The setting is medieval, but the issues addressed have twenty-first century parallels. Pagan's voice—funny, swift, sarcastic, and often touching—carries the novel. This reviewer cannot remember a more compelling or rewarding page-turner. Jinks's writing is a tour de force of young adult prose. Happy are they who read and introduce young readers to Pagan.—Mary E. Heslin.

_____. **Pagan's Crusade**. *Pagan Chronicles*. Candlewick, 2003. 248p. $15.99. 978-0-7636-2019-6. $6.99 Trade pb. 978-0-7636-2584-9.
VOYA December 2003. **5Q · 5P · M · J**

What a romp! Not since Don Quixote took up with Sancho Panza has a knight had a squire like Pagan Kidrouk. In 1187, Muslim forces besiege Crusader-held Jerusalem, but sixteen-year-old Pagan's concerns are more immediate. His life is forfeit if his gambling debts continue unmet, and he enlists with the Knights Templar to stay the creditor's dagger. Assigned as squire to Lord Roland Roucy de Bram, a knight straight out of a "stained-glass window" whose last squire died in battle, Pagan fears he has merely opted for an alternate road to the hereafter. But wisecracking, back-alley-smart, irreverent Pagan is an orphan, and Lord Roland-high-minded, in control, fierce, and noble-becomes a father figure and friend. Whether escorting gullible and often not-so-holy pilgrims to the River Jordan, dealing with corrupt Jerusalem administrators, or treating with the city's besiegers, Pagan and Lord Roland make a formidable team and learn from each other.

Jinks is a medieval scholar, but reader interest in historical fiction is no prerequisite for Pagan. Buy and display this book and its forthcoming three series mates cover out. The art alone will draw teens. Once in, they will relish Pagan's ability to live by his wits and to remain skeptical in the face of secular and religious propaganda. They will also savor his fresh, fast-paced, satirical one-liners and, perchance, identify with the deep-buried vulnerabilities concealed by them.—Mary E. Heslin.

Johnson, Angela. **Sweet, Hereafter**. *Heaven Trilogy*. Simon & Schuster, 2010. $16.99. 978-0-689-87385-0. $7.99 Trade pb. 978-0-689-87386-7
VOYA February 2010. **5Q · 5P · M · J · S**

In the concluding volume of Johnson's *Heaven* trilogy, Shoogy, who had a supporting role in the other volumes, is center stage. A brilliant, restless, renegade, Shoogy lives in a cabin near Heaven, Ohio, with her boyfriend, Curtis, who shares Shoogy's sense of being boxed into impossible corners. Shoogy ran away from home to relieve some unnamed pressure. She has an arrangement whereby she attends a couple of high school classes while holding down a job. Curtis, an Army Reservist who has already served one tour in Iraq and is being deployed again, is AWOL. Shoogy's friends from the previous two volumes, a charming group of mismatched devoted chums, watch out for Shoogy as she struggles to keep Curtis safe during his desperate downward spiral.

Johnson, award winning author of three Coretta Scott King Awards, as well as a Printz Award and a MacArthur Foundation genius grant, again uses spare, gorgeous, realistically raw language to bring to life a complex teen of great depth and heart.—Beth E. Andersen.

Jordan, Robert. **Knife of Dreams**. *Wheel of Time*. Tor, 2005. 784p. $29.95. 978-0-312-87307-3. $7.99 pb. 978-0-8125-7756-3.
VOYA February 2006. **5Q · 5P · S · A/YA** (SF/F/H)

Book eleven of *The Wheel of Time* series is the beginning of the end. One by one, the threads of the pattern start to weave their way toward the Last Battle. Reality itself is becoming unstable-the dead walk and unnatural things are happening. Perrin allies with the Seanchan and finally rescues his wife who was kidnapped by the Shaido Aiel. Darkfriends among the Seanchan conspire to kill Tuon, but Matt and some Seanchan still loyal to her are able to ward them off. Matt and Tuon also complete their marriage ceremony at long last. Egwene, abducted by the Aes Sedai loyal to Eladia in the last book, takes her battle to the heart of the White Tower. Elayne roots out a group of Darkfriends in Caemlyn, and also secures her place as the Queen of Andor. Rand and some of his companions ward off an attack by ten thousand trollocs, and Nynaeve sets her husband Lan on a path to rally the Borderlands for the Last Battle. Rand then attempts to form a truce with the Seanchan-and ends up capturing one of the Forsaken.

Just as in the rest of the books in his epic saga, Jordan quickly thrusts his reader into his world. Fans of the series will love this entry and will not be disappointed. The plot moves at a quick pace, only slowing a little with Elayne's thread. Beyond that minor flaw, the book is a masterpiece that leaves the reader begging for the next installment.—Patrick Darby, Teen Reviewer.

Karras, Erika V. Shearin. **Mean Chicks, Cliques, and Dirty Tricks: A Real Girl's Guide to Getting Through the Day with Smarts and Style**. Adams Media (57 Littlefield St., Avon, MA 02322), 2004. 144p. PLB $19.60. 978-1-4176-5349-2. Biblio. Further Reading. Appendix.
VOYA December 2004. **5Q · 5P · M · J · S** (NF)

Girls will love this book, carry it around with them, and use code words to apply Karras's labels to other girls at school. Karras talks honestly to her audience about the not-so-nice things that girls and women do to each other. Her straightforward delivery combined with comments from teen girls and a fast quiz at the end of each chapter makes this book very user friendly. She does not talk down to her readers but creates a feeling of a heart-to-heart chat with an experienced friend. Karras looks at the roles girls take on, such as "the snob," "the gossip," and "the teaser" among others, and provides empowerment strategies to help everyone survive this tense time. Besides providing all this wonderful information and cozy delivery, this book validates the experience of young girls growing up in society by telling the reader that her feelings, insecurities, and needs to fit in are all normal. There is also a strong assurance that anyone who wants to change, can.

It is true that the female gender-this reviewer's gender-can play rough. Women and girls backstab, gossip, exclude, and can be downright "witchy." This title sets it out in print for everyone to see. Every teen girl should read this book.—C. J. Bott.

Khoury, Jessica. **Origin**. Razorbill/Penguin, 2012. 394p. $17.99. 978-1-59514-595-6.
VOYA October 2012. **5Q · 5P · J · S**

Should humans live forever? It has taken five generations for scientists in the Little Cam compound to create an immortal human. Pia, the first immortal, has been raised to become a scientist and follow their teachings to create a new immortal race. As soon as she is old enough, she will learn the secrets of Little Cam. On the eve of her seventeenth birthday, she discovers a hole in the fence. She sneaks out into the surrounding forest, in which she has never set foot. There she meets Eio, a handsome boy who makes her question her world, her life, and her dreams.

Khoury pens a unique and engrossing debut novel with a dystopian feel. Pia's life has seemed easy until the eve of her birthday. Out in the Amazon, Pia discovers an entirely new world. Slowly, her eyes are opened to new possibilities that make it hard for her to return to her previous life. Teens will connect with Pia's struggles with authority and her attempts to discover what she wants for herself and her life, instead of blindly following someone else's plans. The danger, action, and romance will keep readers turning the pages.—Jennifer Rummel.

Kimmel, J. L., and David Ceccarelli. **The Yawning Rabbit River Chronicle**. Illus. by David Ceccarelli. Spring Tree, 2012. 296p. $17.99. 978-0-9785007-1-9.
VOYA December 2012. **5Q · 5P · M · J**

This magnificent, three-part tale opens in a once-idyllic forest where the creatures fear for their survival amid a drought so long-standing that none recall ever seeing a river and the dangers of hungry hunters. So desperate are they that a lightning-fast jackrabbit thief undertakes a quest to find the mythological river goddess, Violet, and race her for the river. As he departs, the forest librarian owl reads Violet's story aloud from a very special book. Part two occurs many years later on the estate of absurdly conspicuous consumers, Mr. and Mrs. Miller, the latter of whom hates rain and nature sounds. Their children are twins purchased at a bargain price—the loud, aggressive Ash, deemed "boyish" by parents who discount the sensitive, thoughtful Dusty. A mishap with the past makes Ash evil and infects the Miller house with "soul crawlers, parasites of hate that thrived where evil lurked." Twenty years later, in the adjoining township, part three brings thirteen-year-old Nub Begley, a farmer boy, and female classmate Nil Turner. Their adventures complete the complex tapestry of this rich tale.

In this heartwarming tale, good triumphs over evil, danger threatens every good soul, and history is contained within the pages of an important book that appears throughout. This story will make life-long readers of youth not previously committed to reading. Middle schools and public libraries will want multiple copies. Doting adults will do well to gift copies to beloved youth. Adults who take the time to explore these pages will be reminded of the important titles of their youth, the ones that originally hooked them on reading.—Cynthia Winfield.

Korman, Gordon. **Son of the Mob: Hollywood Hustle**. Hyperion, 2004. 272p. PLB $14.99. 978-1-4352-3480-2. $5.99 Trade pb. 978-0-7868-0919-6.
VOYA December 2004. **5Q · 5P · J · S**
Popular Paperbacks for Young Adults 2007.

Vincent Luca is off to college at last. There is no better place for him than at a film school on the other side of the country. California is as far away from New York and his father that Vince can get without leaving the continent. Unfortunately for Vince, one cannot escape the mob that easily. In no time at all, his oldest brother, Tommy, and a flood of "uncles" start appearing at his dorm, armed with trouble and his mother's famous five-cheese baked ziti. Vince is certain that they are not there for a vacation to Disneyland. But Vince has his own problems when his roommate's goddess of a girl-friend starts chasing after the son of the mob. Vince spends his first semester away from home tying to retain his own girlfriend, avoid his roommate's girlfriend, and figure out what his father is up to.

Teens will love this hilarious latest chapter of Vince's life, first encountered in **Son of the Mob** (Hyperion, 2002/**VOYA** February 2003). The complicated plot is neatly bound together by one-liners and awkward situations that Vince cannot seem to avoid, no matter how hard he tries. Each character is portrayed with deft touches of reality that mix perfectly with the clever comedy of errors. It is easy to relate to Vince's problems with his father, friends, and girlfriend. Korman's latest offering is a wonderful sauce filled with brilliant characterization, sneaky plot twists, and humor that will make teens fall off their chairs with laughter.—Leslie McCombs.

Lester, Julius. **Cupid**. Harcourt, 2006. 208p. $17. 978-0-15-202056-9.
VOYA February 2007. **5Q · 5P · M · J · S** (SF/F/H)

Lester again proves his versatility as a writer with a fresh and funny take on classi-cal mythology in his new novel. His Cupid is no sweet-faced cherub but a grown man known for mischief through his well-aimed arrows with potioned tips that can turn even the most powerful of gods on Olympus into puppy-eyed schoolboys. Unfortunately he falls victim to his own prank and finds himself in complete and utter love with Psyche, the beautiful mortal who has summoned the wrath of Venus through no fault of her own. Venus just happens to be Cupid's mother, so he walks a treacherous tightrope between

Venus's desire for revenge and his own desire for Psyche. At this point, Cupid must decide whether to cut the apron strings or stay a momma's boy.

Lester peppers his story with a huge cast of lesser gods that he found while researching Greek and Roman mythology for Cupid stories. In addition, Lester himself becomes a character as narrator, sharing the wisdom he has gained over many decades of love, marriage, and divorce in a voice that is at times the helpful elder and at others the front-porch storyteller. Readers of the classic tales will find the familiar elements all here-the tests, the journey, trickery, divine intervention, and the groupings of three-but they will delight in the contemporary updates and Lester's witty commentary throughout.—Michele Winship.

_____. **Day of Tears: A Novel in Dialogue**. Jump at the Sun/Hyperion, 2005. 192p. PLB $18.40. 978-1-4177-7242-1. $7.99 pb. 978-1-4231-0409-4.
VOYA June 2005. **5Q · 5P · M · J · S**
Coretta Scott King Award 2006.
Best Books for Young Adults 2006.

Although slavery is studied in history lessons in school, most students never learn about the largest slave auction in American history, which took place on March 3 and 4, 1859, in Savannah, Georgia, an event known as "The Weeping Time." Rather than deliver a third-person narrative in a history-book style, Lester takes names, some fictional and others not, and gives a solemn, heartfelt voice to a cast of people whose lives are affected by slavery and the auction. Plantation slaves tell their stories as do slave owners, abolitionists, and children who grew up in slave and slave-owner families. Through dialogue, memories, and thoughts, the many facets of slavery are presented in a thought-provoking manner. One narrator is a slave who believes that the security of slavery provides him a better life than freedom. No apologies for either the white or black characters are given; instead the reader is given the chance to consider and discuss why the characters feel as they do. Woven into the stories of slavery are themes of devotion, family, humanity, and pre-Civil War zeitgeist in which all men were not equal in the eyes of American law.

By not limiting the book to one viewpoint and by using an alternate format, Lester makes this book highly appealing to all readers. Whether the reader agrees with the characters' thoughts, there is no dispute as to the poetic, lyrical quality of the writing or the inability to feel any one thing about any one of the characters.—Carlisle Kraft Webber.

Lisle, Janet Taylor. **The Crying Rocks**. Atheneum/S & S, 2003. 208p. PLB $17.20. 978-1-4177-1987-7.
VOYA February 2004. **5Q · 5P · M · J · S**

For thirteen-year-old Joelle, the past is a secret that both beckons and repels. Her first five years are lost to her memory, filled only with the strange, unsatisfactory explanations of her adoptive mother, Aunt Mary Louise. Could her birth mother really have sent a young Joelle on a freight train from Chicago, without a caretaker or destination?

Had police really discovered her living out of a box and hunting for cigarette butts at the train depot in her present Rhode Island town? None of it sounds believable to Joelle, but she cannot find the memories needed to refute the story.

Again Lisle demonstrates her skill at creating characters rich with personality. Joelle is edgy and defensive on the outside but internally filled with imaginative longings. Coarse, loquacious Aunt Mary Louise and remote Uncle Vernon provide love and support for Joelle, but they cannot seem to answer her burning questions. Joelle turns to a classmate, affable Carlos, who plants the idea in her head that she might be descended from the mysterious Narragansett Indians. Together they explore the local places of nature connected with Narragansett lore, particularly the terrible Crying Rocks, scene of both ancient and recent horrors. In the end, Joelle's questions find surprising answers, and Carlos learns some hidden truths about his own past. As often happens with novels that pivot on a buried secret, the revealing moments are not quite equal to the anticipation. But it is still an excellent story, sure to attract a wide range of age levels with its combination of historical intrigue, adolescent exploration, and mysteries veiled by time.—Diane Emge.

Llewellyn, Sam. **Lyonesse: The Well Between the Worlds**. Scholastic, 2009. 352p. $17.99. 978-0-439-93469-5. $7.99 pb. 978-0-439-93470-1.
VOYA February 2009. **5Q · 5P · M · J · S** (SF/F/H)

Idris Limpet seems like an ordinary eleven-year-old son from a poor family in an insignificant town. But strangely, some powerful people seem to think he would be better dead. Condemned to death by drowning, he is saved by a mysterious stranger called Ambrose, who travels with him to Wellvale, a large walled city filled with wells that mark rifts between two worlds. The wells are used by men to harvest alien monsters who, like phosphorus, self-combust in air. The wells also spill quantities of well water into Lyonesse that flood and poison the land. Enrolled in a school for "monstergrooms," who tend the monsters until they are used as fuel, Indris discovers that Wellvale has deadly secrets. Sea Eagle, who rules Lyonesse, and her son Dolphin, are forbidden "crosses" between human and monster. Her goal is to have the alien ocean world drown Lyonesse completely. She is also the murderous second wife of the king of Lyonesse, whom she poisoned after killing his first wife. Two infant children of the king were saved and hidden. Indris is one of them, the rightful heir of Lyonesse. How can he claim his throne and close the wells between the worlds?

Seldom does one find a new fantasy that is so richly textured, so original in concept, and with such a wonderfully interesting story. Llewellyn creates characters that live on the page. Fantasy lovers will be impatient to find out where their paths take them. — Rayna Patton.

Lu, Marie. **Legend**. Putnam/Penguin, 2011. 336p. $17.99. 978-0-399-25675-2.
VOYA October 2011. **5Q · 5P · J · S**
Best Fiction for Young Adults 2012.
Quick Picks Nomination 2012.
YALSA Readers' Choice List 2013

Day is just fifteen years old, but he is the Republic's most wanted criminal. Day opted out of society after failing his Trial at age ten, and since has launched an attack for survival that the Republic views as treasonous. Despite the presence of surveillance cameras in every corner of the city, the Republic has no image of Day to broadcast over sector JumboTrons. Little wonder, then, that the Republic puts recruits from a premiere military family on Day's case. When Captain Metias Iparis is killed—possibly by Day—his sister June must continue the hunt on her own, while mourning her brother. Commander Jameson has supreme confidence in June, since she scored a perfect 1500 on her Trial.

The themes of Legend—fairness and rebellion—will resonate with a broad range of teens and tweens, providing them a well-written, emotionally satisfying read. A fast-paced blend of action and science fiction (with only a hint of potential romance) means that this one will likely appeal to male and female readers alike. Debut author Lu has managed a great feat—emulating a highly successful young adult series while staying true to her own voice. Legend will give Hunger Games fans something worthwhile to read while they await Katniss' movie debut—and, most likely, Day and June's.—Anna Foote.

Lynch, Chris. **Hothouse**. HarperTeen, 2010. 208p. $16.99. 978-0-06-167379-5.
VOYA October 2010. **5Q · 5P · M · J · S**
Best Fiction for Young Adults 2011.

In **Hothouse**, Lynch has once again masterfully introduced the reader into the very depths of the young male psyche. This time our young hero is actually an ordinary—or possibly extraordinary—high school senior who must face the truth about the dad he has idolized. Russell's father, like his friend D.J.'s father across the street, is a fireman. Brave, loyal, bigger-than-life, they even sport the trademark handlebar moustaches. When both are killed fighting a blaze in a local house fire, the boys must face sharing the loss with the entire community who want to make them heroes. After the investigation suggests that both men may have been using drugs and alcohol on the night in question, they are instantly seen as villains. Struggling to maintain their own sense of self, separate from their family, is proving to be more difficult than imagined.

Weaving tough topics, such as death, friendship, family, school, and identity into a seamless story truthfully portrayed has become Lynch's standard. The reader is soon engulfed in the smooth flow of the story and immediately cares about characters that jump to life, making this an easy book to recommend to almost any reader. **Hothouse** is a satisfying read, beginning to end.—Angie Hammond.

MacHale, D. J. **Pendragon: The Pilgrims of Rayne**. Simon & Schuster, 2007. 560p. $17.99. 978-1-4169-1416-7. PLB $8.99. 978-1-4169-1417-4.
VOYA August 2007. **5Q · 5P · M · J · S** (SF/F/H)

Fans of Bobby Pendragon have been circling the library like hungry sharks, waiting for this eighth volume of the series. It will not disappoint, packed again with nonstop action, mind-boggling plot twists, and well-imagined locales. Bobby and Courtney travel to First Earth to stop Mark, who has fallen under the influence of Saint Dane, from inventing the robot killing machines that infect the future of all of the worlds of Halla. Saint Dane, however, is one step ahead and lures Bobby away to the mysterious island of Ibara. Courtney is left to save Mark on her own, in a world in which she has little clue how to behave. Bobby realizes that he must begin to play the game by Saint Dane's rules if he and Halla are to survive. The Convergence draws near, and Bobby is growing desperate to stop the evil that is slowly engulfing the Territories.

MacHale gives readers a new, darker Pendragon, one who breaks rules, fights to kill, and sadly loses faith in himself and all hope of ever defeating Saint Dane. The tone is grimmer, there is more violence, and the body count is higher than in any of the previous volumes. Courtney, however, finally gets to shine as she embarks on an equally desperate quest of her own. The final showdown is being set up, and the author is taking no prisoners. The book ends on a twist so stunning that those shark-like fans will be back in full force, begging for volume nine.—Arlene Garcia.

McNamee, Graham. **Acceleration**. Random House, 2003. 176p. PLB $15.50. 978-1-4352-9974-0. $6.99 pb. 978-0-440-23836-2.
VOYA December 2003. **5Q · 5P · J · S**
Edgar Award 2004.
Best Books for Young Adults 2004.
Quick Picks for Reluctant Readers 2004.
Popular Paperbacks for Young Adults 2011.
The Ultimate YA Bookshelf

McNamee, author of **Hate You** (Delacorte, 1999/**VOYA** April 1999), pulls no punches in this thriller that moves as fast as trains thundering above the Toronto Transit Commission's lost and found, where seventeen-year-old Duncan finds the journal of a psychopathic killer who is stalking female victims on the subway. At first Duncan just wants to get rid of it, even tries giving it to the police, but he decides that stopping this guy might redeem him from his guilt over not saving a drowning victim the summer before. Duncan and his physically handicapped friend, Vinny, research serial killers at the library. They certainly do not expect the killer, whom they call "Roach," to show up looking for his journal, but he does. Duncan follows Roach home, and then calls his "light-fingered" friend, Wayne, to help him break into the killer's house while he is gone. When Roach finds Duncan in his basement, Duncan escapes only to be caught at the subway station and thrown onto the tracks. In a final attempt to save himself and the girls, Duncan rolls under the platform ledge and grabs Roach's leg, toppling him in front of the oncoming train. While in the hospital with multiple head wounds, Duncan fakes amnesia when police question him about the dead guy. Only Duncan and his buddies know that they stopped a serial killer and released Duncan from his nightmares.

This novel will intrigue Silence of the Lamb fans, but McNamee offers much more. The dark symbolism surrounding the subway and the rich character development are as intoxicating as the adrenalin rush.—Ruth E. Cox.

Marr, Melissa. **Carnival of Souls**. HarperCollins, 2012. 320p. $17.99. 978-0-06-165928-7.
VOYA August 2012. **5Q · 5P · S**
Mallory's life is not that of a typical teenager. Her father, a witch, long ago fled The City in order to stay alive. He has stayed in the human world in order to raise Mallory and teach her skills to keep her from harm. The daimons, deadly shape-shifters who inhabit The City, will be coming for Mallory, and she must fight. Mallory knows little of The City or daimons, and what she does not know will hurt her. The boy she likes, Kaleb, is, in fact, under contract to kill her. As a lower-class daimon, Kaleb's life has not been an easy one, and he takes unsavory jobs in order to stay out of poverty. Kaleb's biggest jobs yet might be next to impossible, though—kill Mallory, a girl he soon recognizes as not human, but daimon, and win The City's fight-to-the-death tournament. Kaleb and Mallory's lives collide in a spectacular tangle of love, hate, and long-standing vendettas.

Marr's talent for blending several story lines together does not fail her here. If this were simply Mallory's story it would be a good book, but the interweaving of the stories of Kaleb, Mallory, and other major players, both in The City and the human world, adds a unique depth to the tale. Add in class warfare, a deadly tournament, and The Carnival of Souls, where any pleasure or contract can be fulfilled, and this is one novel that will be at the top of everyone's to-read list.—Amanda Fensch.

Meloy, Colin. **Wildwood**. Illus. by Carson Ellis. Balzer + Bray, 2011. 560p. $17.99. 978-0-06-202468-8.
VOYA August 2011. **5Q · 5P · M · J · S**
Forest Park in Portland, Oregon, serves as the inspiration for this fantasy collaboration between writer/musician Colin Meloy and his illustrator wife, Carson Ellis. Twelve-year-old Prue, a budding ornithologist, is tasked with caring for her infant brother, Mac. She takes him to the playground, where much to her horror, a murder of crows descends and carries him off into the Impassable Wilderness. Afraid to reveal the truth to her parents, Prue returns home to stock up on essentials before bicycling off to search for Mac. Along the way, she encounters nerdy outcast classmate Curtis, who insists on accompanying her. Prue and Curtis find themselves in the country of Wildwood, where anthropomorphic animals co-exist with magic-touched humans. The pair becomes separated when coyote soldiers abduct Curtis. Prue, clearly an Outsider, must solicit help from various denizens of the forest world, including a human postmaster, a crown prince owl, equality-minded bandits, and mystics who communicate with plants. As the story continues, Prue and Curtis come to realize that they have the power to affect the very survival of Wildwood.

Fantasy lovers of all ages will be enthralled by fast-moving plot lines, evocative descriptions, and smart, snappy dialogue. Readers will find elements of themselves in Prue and Curtis, adolescents for whom the quest to find and rescue Mac is also a journey of self-discovery. The superbly imagined Dowager Governess claims a place at the table for classic, manipulative villains alongside C. S. Lewis's White Witch in the *Chronicles of Narnia* stories and Phillip Pullman's Mrs. Coulter in the *His Dark Materials* series. Meloy smartly weaves realism and the otherworldly, building suspense and adding elements of surprise as the novel comes to a satisfying conclusion. Ellis's trademark detailed ink–and-gouache illustrations draw the reader deeper into this fully realized world. While **Wildwood** is the rare fantasy novel that acts as a stand-alone story, readers will be clamoring for the next installment in this proposed series.—Paula J. Gallagher.

Meyer, Marissa. **Cinder**. *The Lunar Chronicles*. Feiwel & Friends/Macmillan, 2012. 400p. $17.99. 978-0-312-64189-4.
   VOYA December 2011. **5Q · 5P · J · S**
   YALSA Readers' Choice List 2013
   Cinder isn't fully human. For reasons unknown to her, Cinder's body was "altered" when she was eleven years-old, so that now she has a steel mechanical hand and foot; software interlaced throughout her brain; and a heart partially comprised of silicon. Cinder is deeply ashamed of these artificial elements of her body, which place her in the despised social class of a cyborg. She lives in the Eastern Commonwealth, formed after the devastation of World War IV, working as a mechanic and living with her stepmother. Of course, Cinder's stepmother is cruel, and of course, Cinder has two stepsisters. The handsome, unmarried Prince Kai somehow finds Cinder attractive, and begs her to accompany him to the upcoming ball in his honor.
   Readers know the elements of the story before they open the book. What they do not know until they begin turning the pages of this fable-turned-dystopian-science-fiction novel, is that Meyer's embellishments create a spellbinding story of their own. Cinder's world is comprised of androids (some with surprisingly plucky personalities), a highly infectious plague that causes gross mutilation in victims before their swift death, and the threat of invasion from an evil queen who rules the creatures of the moon. The book will appeal to fans of twisted fairy tales, techno-thrillers, romance novels, and well-plotted suspense. Although the happy ending beckons, the story does not end with the final pages, a welcome promise that Cinder will return with more unimagined chapters in a story as old as time.—Diane Colson.

Miranda, Megan. **Hysteria**. Walker/Bloomsbury, 2013. 336p. $17.99. 978-0-8027-2310-9.
   VOYA December 2012. **5Q · 5P · M · J · S · A/YA**
   Mallory killed her boyfriend Brian, and now everyone is wondering if she took every possible step to protect herself before resorting to murder. Brian's mother broke mentally and is stalking her. Even her parents are viewing her with suspicion, so she leaves her past—including loyal best friend Colleen—and flees to Monroe Prep School,

seeking a fresh start. There, she reconnects with Reid, an old family friend and potential love interest. But there are signs that Brian's mother—or someone else, or some*thing* else—has followed her to school. As danger closes in from every corner, readers start to get hints that maybe everything about that night is not as simple as it appears. Furthermore, Monroe may not be the safe haven for which Mallory was hoping. The past has a way of refusing to remain buried.

Also the author of **Fracture** (Walker, 2012/**VOYA** December 2011), Miranda offers a compelling psychological thriller with a heroine who might not be all that innocent. Everything builds to a breath-capturing climax that will have the reader realizing just how invested they are in the characters' fates. Tightly balanced between can't-put-it-down drama and realism, the cherry on top is Miranda's wry writing. For example, Mallory observes that her mother long promised she would never send her daughter to Monroe, decreeing it would happen over her dead body. "Apparently, any dead body would do," Mallory quips. There is really nothing that has not been done in umpteen, empty, slasher/thrillers; yet here, it all feels fresh, addicting, and smart.—Matthew Weaver.

Morkes, Andrew, Ed. **They Teach That in College!? A Resource Guide to More Than 75 Interesting College Majors and Programs**. College and Career Press, 2006. 310p. $19.95 Trade pb. 978-0-9745251-1-2. Index.
VOYA August 2006. **5Q · 5P · M · J · S** (NF)

Got teens in your library? Get this book. If students want a career that taps into today's "ripped from the headlines" immediacy, this resource is the one for them. Crime scene investigations, homeland security, and sustainability are just a few of the areas of study covered. Other chapters highlight institutions of higher learning that are unique in their focus, such as Beacon College, designed for students with learning disabilities. The majors discussed fit three criteria: They fill a job market demand and offer a good salary; no more than 25 percent of the nation's colleges and universities offer the major; and they have to be fun. Chapter layouts are crisp and thorough. An introductory paragraph describing the major makes for enticing reading-how many teens know what bioinformatics or packaging science is? Possible fields of study or available courses follow the introductions. Potential employers and colleges and universities that offer these majors precede lists of relevant organizations that provide more information. Also included are dozens of interviews with key figures in the field. Three indexes-School, Schools by State, and Association/Organization-can help quickly narrow the search. This title is the perfect guide for college-inclined students who are not drawn to the traditional disciplines but do not have a clue where to concentrate. More than one parent is going to wish that they had had such a resource when they were college-bound. They may even find themselves pursuing a second career. This invaluable resource for guidance counselors, school media centers, parents, and the students themselves is highly recommended.—Beth E. Andersen.

Morton-Shaw, Christine. **The Riddles of Epsilon**. Katherine Tegen Books/HarperCollins, 2005. 373p. PLB $17.89. 978-0-06-072820-5. $7.99 pb. 978-0-06-072821-2.

VOYA June 2005. **5Q · 5P · M · J · S** (SF/F/H)

Jess has problems. Her mother has just had an affair, Jess has been expelled from school, and her father's answer to everything is to withdraw into his photography. She has no idea why anyone thinks that a summer spent in a gloomy old house on a small island off the coast of England will solve anything, and Jess is determined to be as unhelpful as possible. Then she stumbles upon an abandoned cottage and thinks that it will be the perfect place to which she can escape-until she finds that it is already occupied by a spirit called Epsilon. Epsilon warns Jess that she and her family are in great danger, for an ancient evil is planning to return to the island. Jess races against time to find the clues that will lead them to the item sought after by beings both good and vile, with only documents a hundred years old to help her decipher the cryptic messages found at every turn.

Although the plot might sound similar to other fantasy novels abounding today, this debut novel rises above clichés to shine with a voice both fantastic and real. Characters are well developed and intriguing, the atmosphere is tangible, and the pacing causes one's heart to race. Epsilon's clues are tantalizing but not impossible to solve, with the reader putting things together only seconds before Jess does. This book is a stay-up-all-night page-turner that not only offers insight into the nature of evil but also into the meaning of family. It is a highly recommended purchase.—Arlene Garcia.

Muharrar, Aisha. **More Than a Label: Why What You Wear or Who You're With Doesn't Define Who You Are**. Free Spirit, 2002. 144p. PLB $22.95. 978-1-4352-8015-1. Index. Photos. Biblio.

VOYA December 2002. **5Q · 5P · M · J · S** (NF)

Popular Paperbacks for Young Adults 2005.

In this much-needed book on the realities and cruelties of labeling, seventeen-year-old Muharrar provides the right voice. She also has taken great time and effort to include teens from all over this country by using more than a thousand responses to a Teen Labels Survey that asks why teens use labels, how they feel about them, and what they can do about them. Muharrar interweaves their thoughts with her own great commentary. The survey is included in the front of the book, enabling teens to take it before they read what everyone else thinks. This book speaks to all youth-the ones overwhelmed and molded by their assigned labels, the ones assigning the labels, and the ones embracing their labels. Usually concerned with harassed youth, this reviewer had truly never realized that some actually like their labels. Muharrar also includes informative pages and blocked comments quoted directly from survey responses. The presentation is cleverly and engagingly done.

This book is serious; it is not MTV in print. One chapter, "Slurs and Other Hate Words," is straightforward and gutsy. It alone is worth the price of the book. The whole school community-students, staff, and administration-would benefit from reading this chapter. This book is a win/win purchase-buy it, give it as a gift, read it, discuss it, follow it. Everyone can use the reminders.—C. J. Bott.

Mullin, Mike. **Ashen Winter**. Tanglewood, 2012. 594p. $17.95. 978-1-933718-75-0.
 VOYA October 2012. **5Q · 5P · J · S**

The United States has fallen prey to a super volcano in Yellowstone Park. Alex and Darla fought their way out of FEMA and paramilitary camps to find Alex's family in Illinois, only to find that his parents had gone looking for him. Alex and Darla head out to find them after the farm is attacked by bandits that have Alex's father's gun. Shortly after they set out, Darla is shot and taken captive. Alex roams all over the Midwest in an attempt to get her back. He finds his parents in a FEMA camp that they cannot leave. His parents believe it is their duty to save this camp from "flensers" that are stealing people to use as slaves or to eat. The government is no help. Alex and his parents save the camp with the help of some friends and leave to once again look for Darla. His parents do not seem to understand why he needs to find her. His mother just wants to go home to Illinois, but his father decides to help him find the love of his life. What cost will Alex pay to get Darla back? Is the cost too high? What is going on at home when he returns?

In this sequel to **Ashfall** (Tanglewood, 2011/**VOYA** December 2011), Mullin has outdone himself with nonstop action and injury. Just as soon as you think Alex has it all figured out, the other shoe drops and more problems arise. This book contains some content that may not be suitable for younger readers, such as sex, cannibalism, and violence.—Barbara Allen.

Myers, Walter Dean. **The Dream Bearer**. HarperCollins, 2003. 240p. PLB $16.89. 978-0-06-029522-6. $5.99 pb. 978-0-06-447289-0.
 VOYA June 2003. **5Q · 5P · M · J**

Imagine a book about a twelve-year-old boy, David, and his best friend, Loren. Sometimes they fight, but mostly they just hang together, being there for each other through good and bad. Imagine a book about a family-worn-out, hardworking mom; a teenage son spending too much time out on the streets; a father struggling against mental illness; and David, the youngest who loves them all. Now imagine a book about a community, Harlem, and its fight for a safe, clean neighborhood that reflects the commitment and integrity of the people who have walked its streets for generations. Finally, imagine a book about African American people and their dreams-the sad, sad dreams of the past and current dreams of hope that preserve the dreams of the future.

Roll all of these imaginings together for a sense of Myers's story. This incredible novel, written in easy, natural language suitable for the younger middle school crowd, tells many large and small stories, all through the eyes of young David. Readers learn how handsome Loren's doting white mother really feels about living in Harlem, for example, and how the neighbors react to David's friend Sessi and her family, who have just emigrated from Africa. They observe the dignity of homeless Mr. Moses, the dream bearer, who claims to be more than three hundred years old, and the undulating tension between David's parents, trying to redeem a marriage conflicted with internal and external catastrophes. This book comprises many stories, beautifully orchestrated with elegant simplicity and profound insight. Myers creates a real masterpiece with this one.—Diane Masla.

Naylor, Phyllis Reynolds. **The Grooming of Alice**. Simon & Schuster, 2001, ©2000. 224p. $4.99 pb. 978-0-689-84618-2.
VOYA October 2000. **5Q · 5P · M · J**

This twelfth book in the Alice series is just as enjoyable as the first. Those readers who have watched Alice growing up since Naylor began the series in 1985 with **The Agony of Alice** (Atheneum) feel as if she is a sister/friend/daughter/niece. This installment takes place during the summer between eighth and ninth grades, and Alice is still seeing Patrick. Alice and her best friends, Pamela and Elizabeth, decide to get into shape by running every morning. Pamela, who is dealing with her parents' recent divorce, becomes obsessed and begins to show symptoms of anorexia. Pamela eventually runs away from home, and by helping her, Alice gets them both in trouble. Alice's summer volunteer position at the hospital forces her to deal with the death of a favorite former teacher, which in turn causes her to worry when her brother and father go on vacation.

Of course, these events are not all that occurs within the pages of this volume. As usual, Alice's father and brother each have their own adventures, which have an impact on Alice. Alice comes to realize that her actions have an effect on them as well. Naylor again succeeds in packing a lot of activity into this book while still managing to write a realistic, engaging novel.—Marlyn Roberts.

Nimmo, Jenny. **Charlie Bone and the Time Twister**. *Children of the Red King*. Orchard, 2003. 416p. $12.99. 978-0-439-49687-2.
VOYA February 2004. **5Q · 5P · M · J · S** (SF/F/H)

In the second book of this entrancing series after **Midnight for Charlie Bone** (Orchard, 2003/**VOYA** August 2003), Charlie meets his great uncle Henry Yewbeam. When they were young boys, Ezekiel Bloor's hatred for the Yewbeam family led to calamity. Without warning, Henry found himself twisting through time and space to the present on the day that Ezekiel rolled a strikingly unusual marble into the ring and Henry was unable to take his eyes off the swirling colors. Ezekiel, now an old, sick man, is still determined to get rid of "young" Henry once and for all. That plot is spoiled when the marble rolls into the hands of Mrs. Bloor. A gifted violinist, she has lived in pain and isolation ever since son Manfred smashed her fingers by slamming a door on her hand. She joyfully uses the time twister to return to a time before the assault and a new life in Paris far away from her dreadful family. Meanwhile, Henry has been imprisoned by the Bloors. Charlie and his endowed friends come to their rescue. Their abilities to create storms, fly, and even converse with people in portraits result in a successful deliverance. The schemes of the Bloors and Charlie's detestable aunts are thwarted again as Henry is reunited with his younger brother, James.

Through unique characters who stand apart from inimitable comparisons to counterparts in *Harry Potter* books, Nimmo skillfully creates an exemplary series that stands on its own. Anticipation for readers is building as Charlie moves closer to discovering his "missing-in-plain-sight-although-no-one-realizes-it" father.—Pam Carlson.

Palma, Felix J. **The Map of Time**. Atria/Simon & Schuster. 624p. $26. 978-1-4391-6739-7.

VOYA Online August 2011. **5Q · 5P · S**

Readers will jump easily into **The Map of Time**, especially as the first sentence has one of the main characters selecting a gun with which to kill himself—but the decision is not easy (for many reasons), and soon Andrew finds himself time traveling to the home of H.G. Wells himself to "investigate purported incidents of time travel and to save lives and literary classics." Felix J. Palma has created a gripping historical fantasy that mingles fictional characters with real ones in Victorian London, and has created a real sense of time travel for 21st-century readers. This is Palma's first work to be translated into English, and it has been a hit in the United Kingdom.

The book is divided into three parts, each almost a separate novel. Each has a different flavor, story, and hero. Each part also picks up threads from the others, and if readers think they know what is going on in one section, the next is sure to turn everything upside down. This thick tome (coming in at just over six hundred pages) is a thrilling page-turner—from Victorian England to Jack the Ripper to missing moments by mere seconds, teens (and adults alike) will be intrigued by the lyrical storytelling and the extreme attention to detail that glues together this intense thriller which asks the question: What happens if we change history?—Ria Newhouse.

Paterson, Katherine. **The Same Stuff as Stars**. Clarion, 2002. 256p. $15. 978-0-618-24744-8. PLB $15.99. 978-1-4352-9874-3. $8.99 Trade pb.

VOYA October 2002. **5Q · 5P · M · J**

Angel Morgan is in trouble. Her daddy is in jail, her mama has disappeared, and her great-grandma needs a mother almost more than she does. As with the main character in Cynthia Voigt's **Dicey's Song** (Atheneum, 1982), eleven-year-old Angel is a child forced to be an adult, mothering her aggravating seven-year-old brother, Bernie; cajoling her great-grandma into acting like a grown-up; and desperately trying to stay out of foster care. Angel's only breaks from her constant worrying are her midnight visits to the pasture behind her great-grandma's house. There the mysterious Star Man lets her look through his telescope and teaches her about astronomy. Her visits to the village library also help, as bent and crooked Miss Liza supplies her with books and the kind of information a kid trying to be a grown-up tends to need. Somebody tells Angel, "Sometimes trouble comes piling in." She surely knows it. First her mama steals Bernie away and Angel fears for his safety, then the Star Man disappears, and finally Angel's daddy shows up wanting her to go with him. It just gets worse from there.

Paterson's deft hand at characterization, her insight into the human soul, and her glorious prose make this book one to rejoice over. She portrays Angel's relationship with her brother and great grandmother so convincingly, so heartbreakingly, that they become more real than life itself. Although the odds are stacked mile-high against the resilient Angel and her life will never be easy, this book is hopeful, one that should be on every library shelf.—Rebecca Barnhouse.

Paver, Michelle. **Ghost Hunter: Chronicles of Ancient Darkness**. HarperCollins Children's Books, 2010. 304p. $16.99. 978-0-06-072840-3. PLB $17.89. 978-0-06-072841-0. $6.99 pb. 978-0-06-072842-7.
VOYA October 2010. **5Q · 5P · M · J · S** (SF/F/H)
Guardian Award 2010.

A strange sleeping sickness decimates the woodland clans. Moths gather in odd clusters, their dust virulent and deadly. Torak, tormented by visions of his dead father, recognizes Eostra's work and sets out to find the Eagle Owl Mage in the mountains. He watches a huge Eagle Owl land near Darkfur and her pups but arrives too late to save them—Darkfur falls off a cliff, into the raging river below. One pup, Shadow, is killed, and the Owl flies off with Pebble in its talons. Wolf is inconsolable. Torak's destiny promises death at Eostra's hands. He goes willingly to meet it, but Renn refuses to let him go alone. Old friends appear to ease their journey. In a terrifying battle in the depths of the mountains, Torak destroys Eostra but sacrifices himself. Only Wolf's undying devotion coaxes Torak's spirit back to his body and brings him back to life.

Paver has produced this six-book series without a misstep. The primitive setting imparts timelessness to both characters and plot, ensuring their continued popularity. Her impeccable research is evident in every detail and lends unusual authenticity to her work. Consistent writing, nonstop action, and endearing characters set these books apart. Although a great many readers will be sad to see this series end, the bittersweet conclusion is both satisfying and realistic: Wolf finds Darkfur and Pebble injured but alive, and Renn forsakes her own clan to leave with Torak. This innovative series has earned a place in every school and public library.—Nancy Wallace.

Peck, Richard. **Fair Weather**. Dial, 2001. 160p. $16.99. 978-0-8037-2516-4. $6.99 pb. 978-0-439-43034-0.
VOYA October 2001. **5Q · 5P · M · J**
Best Books for Young Adults 2002.

Following closely on the heels of his Newbery-winning **A Year Down Yonder** (Dial, 2000/**VOYA** December 2000), Peck's newest charmer is set again in the author's home state of Illinois. Studded with unforgettable characters, this story follows three children, who never have been off the family farm, as they travel by train with their high-spirited, ingenuous grandfather to the great city of Chicago to visit the 1893 World's Columbian Exposition. They stay with their mother's sister, Aunt Euterpe, and in her company, uncontrollable disasters seem to occur. The widow of a successful businessman, Aunt Euterpe's fervent desire is to become accepted in Chicago society. To this end, she calculates every stop at the fair, every piece of clothing, and every encounter for her visitors. To her horror, the children, and especially her father, insist on having fun. Over the course of a few days, Euterpe's rural relatives manage to run off the cook and maid, glimpse bad women on the Midway, and horrify Mrs. Potter Palmer, cream of the society ladies. Grandfather and the kids find it all exhilarating, and in an all's-well-that-ends-well fashion, Aunt Euterpe finally is accepted into South Side society when her oldest niece from the farm marries into the Dearborn family.

Readers will find themselves laughing out loud at the antics of this family as seen through the eyes of thirteen-year-old Rosie, and they will feel that they are participants at the fair with all its amazing wonders. This book will provide excellent supplemental reading for studies of the Gilded Age and will be popular with all Peck fans.—Leslie Carter.

Peters, Julie Anne. **Keeping You a Secret**. Little, Brown, 2005, ©2003. 250p. $7.99 Trade pb.
VOYA June 2003. **5Q · 5P · J · S**
Popular Paperbacks for Young Adults 2006.

Anyone who has ever fallen in love will recognize themselves in the realistic characters of this captivating love story. Holland Jaeger, high school senior and student council president, is comfortable with the status quo. She has a steady boyfriend, Seth, and her mother, who dropped out of high school to have Holland, pushes the college applications that Holland is avoiding. When the new student, Cecelia Goddard, catches her eye, Holland's world is soon turned upside down. Cece's IMRU? T-shirt with a rainbow triangle is Holland's first clue that any students at Southglenn High might be gay-let alone out and proud. Although Cece permeates her thoughts and dreams, Holland is unready to acknowledge the attraction. Adolescent pains multiply when Holland does not want to hurt Seth, but she realizes that their relationship is over. How will others close to her react to Holland's new lesbian identity?

Readers will anticipate, cringe, laugh, and cry along as Holland grows into her new love and new life. When her mother overreacts, readers realize that the story is not atypical for gay youth. Not just a gay love story, this book transcends barriers, allowing readers of all persuasions to revel in its universal truths about self-knowledge, acceptance, pride, and the hardships of wrestling with the perceptions and comfort of others. There is no graphic sex but excessive excitement of new love that is right; however, although Holland's mother monitors her birth control pills, there is no mention of safe sex.—Cynthia Winfield.

Picoult, Jodi, and Samantha Van Leer. **Between the Lines**. Simon Pulse, 2012. 368p. $19.99. 978-1-4516-3575-1.
VOYA June 2012. **5Q · 5P · M · J · S**

Fairy tales are just that: tales. But the characters in **Between the Lines** have their own lives when the book is closed. Oliver longs to escape his prescribed existence in the book, and Delilah is obsessed with Oliver's book. She reads it constantly because she feels a connection with Oliver since he too grew up without his father. One day Oliver realizes that Delilah can hear him, and they strike up a friendship. The two long to find a way for Oliver to leave the book. The first attempts backfire when only words will leave the book and every time the book is shut everything starts back at square one. Delilah's mother begins to think something is wrong because Delilah will not stop reading this fairy tale and is talking to the book. In a last-ditch effort, Delilah travels to the author's house to see if she can find a way to safely remove Oliver from the book.

Picoult and her daughter, Van Leer, have created a multilayered universe where what is real is in the eye of the beholder. All at once, the reader is in the fairy tale, in the world of the book when it is closed, and outside the book. Delilah and Oliver allow the reader to suspend their realities and hope that Oliver finds a way to live outside his predestined world and be with the girl of his dreams.—Barbara Allen.

Pierce, Tamora. **Lady Knight**. *Protector of the Small*. Random House, 2002. 448p. $16.60 Trade pb. 978-0-375-82908-6. $7.50 pb. 978-0-375-81471-6.
    VOYA February 2003. **5Q · 5P · M · J · S** (SF/F/H)
    This eagerly awaited fourth and final book in the *Protector of the Small* series will not disappoint Pierce's many fans. Keladry of Mindelan is one of two lady knights in all the kingdom of Tortall. Tortall and its neighbor Scanra are engaged in military conflict, and Kel joins Tortall's armies near the shared border. Upon arriving, Kel does not receive a battle assignment as she had hoped, but the command of a refugee camp instead, a task not to her liking. Nevertheless, with Scanra's phantom killing machines on the rampage, Kel discovers her talents for compassion and diplomacy are needed to safeguard the war's victims. In a wrenching conclusion, Kel must choose between the army and her refugees, when a Scanran mage kidnaps refugee children and Kel's superiors order her to abandon the refugees to a murderous enchantment. Disobeying orders, Kel attempts a perilous rescue whose outcome brings the series to a well-paced conclusion.
    Unrelentingly realistic in its depiction of the horrors of war, this novel draws the reader into a complete and believable fantasy world. Pierce provides exquisite details of the weaponry, topography, and culture of her world, and her control of a voluminous cast of characters is masterful. Readers will be gratified by Pierce's ability to develop Kel's maturing personality, as well as those of characters from previous novels. Hand this chunky novel to your resident Pierce readers and watch them devour it gleefully. Every teen collection should stock this title.—Caitlin Augusta.

_____. **Melting Stones**. *Circle Reforged*. Scholastic, 2008. 320p. $17.99. 978-0-545-05264-1. $8.99 pb. 978-0-545-05265-8.
    VOYA December 2008. **5Q · 5P · M · J** (SF/F/H)
    Pierce returns to the world of her *Circle of Magic* and *Circle Opens* quartets for a first-of-a-kind publishing event. She wrote this novel in audiobook format, which was beautifully recorded by Full Cast Audio (2007/AudioTalk, **VOYA** April 2008) a year before the print version became available. Central here is Evvy, the street urchin Briar rescued in **Street Magic** (Scholastic, 2001/**VOYA** April 2001), the second book of *The Circle Opens*. Four years have passed, and Evvy is in training as a stone mage at Winding Circle Temple. Now fourteen, she accompanies Rosethorn, with her plant magic, and Myrrhtide, a disapproving Water Mage, on their mission to Starns, an island where plants are dying and water is being poisoned. Evvy and her living rock companion, Luvo, the heart of a mountain, uncover the cause, a deadly threat to the continued existence of the island. Evvy barely survives her meeting with volcano spirits who are determined to break free from their underground confinement and reach the surface, no matter how much death and destruction follows. She and the other mages have their

hands full, trying to convince the stubborn inhabitants of the island to flee. And when time runs out, it is up to Evvy to save the day, a Pierce "sheroe" who does not sit around waiting to be saved but goes out and does the saving herself.

Fans old and new are going to love Evvy's adventures-in both formats-whether or not they have read the other *Circle* books.—Bonnie Kunzel.

Poe, Edgar Allan. **Tales of Terror**. Illus. by Michael McCurdy. Knopf, 2005. 96p. PLB $17.99. 978-0-375-93305-9. Illus.
VOYA December 2005. **5Q · 5P · J · S** (SF/F/H)

With haunting black-and-white illustrations, McCurdy creates a dramatic context for six of Poe's psychological and sometimes supernatural thrillers. A biographical introduction outlines the "strange and tragic" life that produced Poe's masterpieces and his place in American literary history. An excellent note establishing historical context introduces each story and suggests Poe's possible sources of inspiration that encompass war, sickness, crime, and perversion. The longer tales are "The Pit and the Pendulum" and "The Fall of the House of Usher". The shorter selections, "The Masque of the Red Death", "The Black Cat", "The Tell-Tale Heart", and "The Cask of Amontillado", are also included on a free CD accompanying the book. (The CD was not packaged with the review copy.)

The cover, size, and graphics will entice young and old readers to acquaint or reacquaint themselves with "the master of the horror story and the father of the modern detective thriller." If the CD maintains the quality of the text, this edition of Poe will spend most of its time off the shelves.—Lucy Schall.

Pullman, Philip. **Amber Spyglass**. *His Dark Materials*. Knopf/Random House, 2000. $7.50 Trade pb. 978-0-440-41856-6. $7.50 pb. 978-0-440-23815-7.
VOYA December 2000. **5Q · 5P · M · J · S** (SF/F/H)
Best Books for Young Adults 2002.

A legion of readers can at last immerse themselves in the final volume of Pullman's *His Dark Materials* trilogy, a stunning and sophisticated conclusion to the alternate world adventures of pragmatic Will and passionate Lyra, first met in **The Golden Compass** and **The Subtle Knife** (Knopf, 1995 and 1997/combined review **VOYA** June 1998). Immediately the reader is plunged into the story. Lyra and her alter ego/daemon, Pantalaimon, lie in a drugged coma, having been kidnapped by her mother, the magnificently amoral Mrs. Coulter. Will, wounded in body and spirit but still bearing the subtle knife, a fearful instrument that can cut openings between worlds, sets out to find his friend and return her precious alethiometer. Some unusual allies aid Will in his seemingly impossible task: Lyra's comrade, Iorek Byrnison, the great armored bear, and two surprising angels, Balthamos and Baruch. Somehow these two children have a part to play, a role beyond any they might imagine, in the war raging between heaven and Earth. As battles storm around them, Lyra and Will must repay a debt by beginning the most perilous and agonizing journey of all to the dank monochrome world of the dead, where no living creature has ever gone and from whence no one may return.

Pullman introduces some remarkable new characters: the Gallivespians, a race of dashing hand-sized warriors; the mulefa, beings who have reinvented the wheel; No-Name the harpy, horrifying guardian of the door to the land of the dead; and two surprisingly bonded angels. Readers also can renew acquaintance with some of the special characters from the previous books: Lyra's feisty and stubborn daemon, Pan; Lyra's proud and terrifying parents, Lord Asriel and Marisa Coulter; and Mary Malone, the ex-nun and physicit who makes the amber spyglasses to see the enigmatic particles called Dust.

Throughout the book, scenes of mind-numbing terror alternate with quiet vignettes of almost pastoral simplicity. As the forces of the Authority of Heaven and the armies of Earth reenact the story of Milton's **Paradise Lost**, Mary Malone lives in harmony with nature in the universe of the gentle mulefa, and Will and Lyra upset all the laws of heaven and nature on the journey to the dead. It is a measure of Pullman's skill as a writer that the reader moves willingly from world to world, marveling and accepting. The book will be called shocking and, perhaps, too powerful for children. Although the book has many of the trappings of fantasy—talking beasts, travel between worlds, monsters and angels—it is actually about reality, about innocence and experience, and about growing up and making sacrifices. It might not be popular with the fans of Harry Potter and the residents of Hogwarts. Compared to Pullman's characters, Harry and his friends resemble the stuff of Saturday morning cartoons. Like Swift, Shakespeare, and Tolkien, Pullman uses the conventions of fantasy to reveal the most profound reality. Characters change, age, and sometimes die in Pullman's trilogy. Pullman's views on theology—that the Church is vicious and cruel, that God is just another angel, and that the afterlife resembles an internment camp—will bother some readers, but the author remains true to his vision of the trilogy as a retelling of the Temptation, Fall, and Redemption of Man. Great literature, as this trilogy undoubtedly is, cannot be an easy read. It expands the reader's consciousness, helping both spiritual and emotional growth. In these books readers share with Lyra and Will the pain, terror, and joy of growing up.

Powerful and provocative, this ambitious fantasy is arguably the best of the trilogy. The writing is flawless; the imaginative vision is breathtaking; and the conclusion is heartbreaking but fitting and proper. At the close of this masterpiece, the reader can only marvel at Pullman's genius, alternately weeping and rejoicing for one's humanity. All who read it will come away enriched, enlightened, and aching for a daemon of one's own.—Jamie S. Hansen

_____. **Once Upon a Time in the North**. *His Dark Materials*. Knopf, 2008. 112p. $12.99. 978-0-375-84510-9.
VOYA April 2008. **5Q · 5P · M · J** (SF/F/H)

This rip-roaring novella, a prequel to **The Golden Compass** (Knopf, 1995/ **VOYA** June 1998), centers on the Texan balloonist Lee Scoresby, his daemon Hester, and their first meeting with the armored bear Iorek Byrnison. All three are still quite young. Scoresby, who has only recently won his balloon in a card game, can barely land it without crashing, and Iorek has not yet made his armor, making do with a mere helmet. When Scoresby reaches the northern island of Novy Odense, he is looking for nothing more than a short-term job, but what he finds is a case of injustice that he cannot ignore. A crooked politician named Ivan Poliakov and powerful mining business Larsen Manganese have joined forces to take control of the island and corner its oil rights. Poliakov is running for mayor on a hate-filled platform aimed at exterminating the local armored bears and is also trying to force a ship's captain into bankruptcy by impounding his cargo. Moreover he has hired the murderous Pierre McConville, whom Scoresby previously encountered back in Dakota country, to kill anyone who gets in his way.

Featuring appealing characters, an exciting gunfight, insightful political commentary, a variety of mysterious documents similar to those included in Pullman's previous novella, **Lyra's Oxford** (2003/**VOYA** June 2004), and a Chutes-and-Ladders-like arctic adventure board game attached to the back cover of the book, this exciting tale should strongly appeal to the author's many fans.—Michael Levy.

Raven, Nicky, adapter. **Dracula**. Illus. by Anne Yvonne Gilbert. Candlewick Press, 2010. 96p. PLB $19.99. 978-0-7636-4793-3.
VOYA August 2010. **5Q · 5P · S** (SF/F/H)

The prospect of a remake of Bram Stoker's classic is, at first, frightening. This book, however, quickly quells any uneasiness with the first of many gorgeous illustrations. Gilbert's artwork is so lushly vivid and lovingly crafted—particularly the recurring bat imagery and a scene where a wolf drinks a young woman's blood—that it threatens to overpower the words altogether. As we advance through a story both familiar and fresh, heroine Mina waits for word from her fiancé, Jonathan, who has gone to Transylvania to help a mysterious Count Dracula arrange housing in London. It's not long before the count has arrived and dear friend Lucy Holmwood falls gravely ill. Mina and Jonathan, with the aid of Professor Abraham Van Helsing, must work to rid themselves of the most famous vampire of all.

Raven has rearranged Stoker's novel and made slight alterations to the story, including the addition of a gypsy boy who bears a long-standing vendetta against the infamous count, and a twist to the ending that would doubtless have sat well with the original author. In the midst of *Twilight* fervor, it must have been tempting to revisit Dracula as a tortured romantic figure, but aside from his new blond locks, there's plenty here to please longtime enthusiasts and welcome a whole new audience to a tale that, just as its central figure, refuses to die.—Matthew Weaver.

Reeve, Philip. **A Darkling Plain**. Eos/HarperCollins, 2007. 978-0-439-94997-2. O.P.
VOYA October 2007. **5Q · 5P · J · S** (SF/F/H)
Guardian Award 2006.

Philip Reeve's four volume *Hungry City Chronicles*, now complete with **A Darkling Plain**, is nothing less than a masterpiece of contemporary young adult science fiction. Set eons from today, on an Earth where our own future has become the ancient past, two great civilizations contest for dominance. First there are the hungry cities of the series title, mobile behemoths that have laid waste to much of the planet in their never-ending obsession with consumption and the unwavering belief in Municipal Darwinism. Then there's the Green

Storm, radical environmentalist who have created monstrous killers called Stalkers, cyborgs from dead human bodies, in their desire to wipe out the mobile cities. In volume one of the series, **Mortal Engines** (HarperCollins, 2001/**VOYA** October 2003), the great city of London, one of the most dangerous predators on the planet, was destroyed when it attempted to recreate a deadly weapon from the past. Surviving the wreck London, apprentice historian Tom Natsworthy and the badly scared but highly competent Hester Shaw went off on a series of adventures. As **A Darkling Plain** opens, years have passed and the couple are now separated, but their daughter Wren has grown to young womanhood and shares her father's life as an itinerant aviator trading among the traveling cities. Unbeknownst to them, Stalker Fang, a monstrous creature fashioned from the remains of a Green Storm heroine, has made the decision that the only way to preserve life on Earth is to wipe out all humanity through the deployment of yet another ancient deadly weapon.

Although his primary purpose is to tell a good story—and he succeeds admirably in doing so—Reeve has much to say that is highly critical of both capitalism and such ecoterrorist groups as PETA and the Animal Liberation Front. **A Darkling Plain** is an unforgettable experience, although readers will be best served by taking the four volumes of the series in order.—Michael Levy

Riggs, Ransom. **Miss Peregrine's Home for Peculiar Children**. Quirk, 2011. 352p. $17.99. 978-1-59474-476-1.
VOYA June 2011. **5Q · 5P · M · J · S**
Best Fiction for Young Adults 2012.

"Find the bird. In the loop. On the other side of the old man's grave. September third, 1940." "Emerson—the letter. Tell them what happened, Yacob." A mysterious death, cryptic clues, and unseen monsters haunt Jacob after the brutal death of his grandfather. His fear consumes him until he cannot even leave the house. His therapist suggests a trip to the school where his grandfather was raised after the war that seems to be the source of his confusion. It should provide closure and answers to his questions. But no answers come, only more questions. Can Jacob unravel the clues his grandfather left? Is he crazy or was there really a monster that killed his grandfather? Is the school more than just the burned-out ruins left from the bombing on September 3, 1940? Jacob finds the school and the room that once belonged to his grandfather. Then the children find him and two worlds collide for the first time since his grandfather left the school. Secrets are exposed and monsters revealed.

Riggs delves into an edge-of-your-seat adventure exploring a world just below the surface of our own, only frozen in time to save the children from the dangers that surround them. With real vintage photos of the "peculiar" children and action-packed text, this is sure to get even your most reluctant reader to whiz through the pages.—Barbara Allen.

Riordan, Rick. **The Son of Neptune: The Heroes of Olympus, Book Two**. Hyperion, 2011. 544p. $19.99. 978-1-4231-4059-7.
VOYA February 2012. **5Q · 5P · M · J**

Riordan's original demigod hero returns to the spotlight in this highly anticipated second book in the *Heroes of Olympus* series. With two indestructible gorgons hunting him, an amnesiac Percy Jackson arrives at Camp Jupiter, the Roman equivalent of the secret Greek demigod camp, Camp Half-Blood. There he learns that Death has been imprisoned and that the titan Gaea is assembling an army of escaped souls and immortal monsters to reclaim the world from the gods. Percy embarks on a seemingly impossible quest to free Death before Gaea's army obliterates Camp Jupiter. At his side are two new Roman friends: Hazel Levesque, who conceals mysteries about her past, and Frank Zhang, who wonders about his immortal lineage and likewise harbors his own secrets. Together they journey to the land beyond the gods to fulfill a prophecy and to each assume a role as one of the seven heroes of Olympus.

Riordan's seamless weaving of various cultural mythologies into a modern landscape continues to shine in **Son of Neptune**. As in previous books, the plot is engrossing, the characters robust and compelling. Percy, Frank, and Hazel alternate as narrators without missing a beat of pace, suspense, or humor. Readers will find themselves automatically consumed by the story without having read the first book, though some knowledge of Percy's previous adventures will help fill in minor gaps of background information. **Son of Neptune** is yet another absorbing and exciting addition to Riordan's chronicles.—Grace Enriquez.

Rogasky, Barbara. **Smoke and Ashes: The Story of the Holocaust**. Revised and expanded ed. Holiday House, 2002, ©1988. 256p. 978-0-8234-1612-7. O.P. Glossary. Index. Illus. Photos. Maps. Charts. Biblio. Source Notes. Chronology. **VOYA** October 2002. **5Q · 5P · M · J · S** (NF)

Not often does an author get the opportunity to surpass her own work, but Rogasky has done just that. In the wake of the September 11 tragedy, she has added new depth and meaning to her well-reviewed work, first published in 1988, on the causes, effects, and victims of the Holocaust. The most immediately noticeable changes are visual, including a more readable typeface, sharper photographs, and clearer maps. Rogasky no longer identifies countries with female pronouns, and swastikas have been removed as map icons. The book's special dedication reveals Rogasky's own personal losses to Hitler's Final Solution. Most importantly, she demonstrates that present circumstances are fertile ground for similar tragedy. Her concise volume is comprehensive, well researched, and written in a manner that conveys her dedication to her subject matter and its related issues. Homosexual men are now included with the Holocaust's other victims. A new chapter has been added, highlighting the role of British Intelligence in bringing the war to a close. Rogasky relates other genocides, such as those in Bosnia and Rwanda, which have occurred within modern teens' lifetimes. The chapter on hate crimes has been expanded to include the effects and power of the Internet on propagating hate groups and distributing Holocaust denial materials.

Finally, Rogasky uses September 11 to admonish readers to never forget the lessons taught by that first, systematic widespread slaughter. This volume should become a standard, surpassing even Milton Meltzer's classic **Never to Forget** (Harper, 1976) in scope and relevancy.—Arlene Garcia.

Rosen, Jared, and David Rippe. **The Flip: Turn Your World Around!** Hampton Roads, 2006. 247p. $23.95. 978-1-57174-474-6. Index.
VOYA December 2006. **5Q · 5P · · J · S** (NF)

"Imagine yourself on a bridge between two worlds," standing poised to choose one or the other. The Upside-Down world offers stress, war, seemingly insurmountable debt, pollution, crime and violence, poisoned food, and pharmaceutical remedies. The Right-Side Up world is calm, meditative, mindful, nurturing, healthful and organic, and lighthearted. Barry lives in the readily recognizable Upside-Down world; Mary is living in the Right-Side Up world that offers glimpses that readers will recognize and new possibilities. In each chapter, Rosen and Rippe present their unabashedly biased views without preaching, use Barry's and Mary's lives for illustration, converse with four experts or celebrities who have experienced The Flip, and close with "flip tips" for flipping into the Right-Side Up world. Web addresses included throughout the text facilitate further research.

Leaving room for readers to choose, Rosen and Rippe present an impassioned plea for sane and sustainable practices. After recognizing the upside-down aspects of today's world, readers appreciate how easily the Right-Side Up world could be attained. Paced for short attention spans, this comprehensive resource is useful for any content classroom as well as many electives. English classes could examine persuasive argument and comparison. Civics classes might explore societal structures, resource allocation, economics, values systems, and wealth distribution. Science curriculums covering fossil fuels, renewable energy, medical practices, and stressors-planetary and human-could benefit. Investigations of compound interest, exponential growth, ratios and proportions, and the effects of the Federal Reserve and fluctuating interest rates could provide real-life uses for mathematics. Even short, infrequent glimpses will lure readers to the empowering message.—Cynthia Winfield.

Rowling, J. K. **Harry Potter and the Order of the Phoenix**. Harry Potter. Scholastic, 2003. 896p. $29.99. 978-0-439-35806-4. $12.99 Trade pb. 978-0-439-35807-1.
VOYA August 2003. **5Q · 5P · M · J · S** (SF/F/H)
Teens Top Ten 2004.
Best Books for Young Adults 2004.
Mythopoeic Fantasy Award 2008.

Denying Voldemort's alleged return to power, the Ministry of Magic sets out to discredit Harry's supporters, including Dumbledore's Order of the Phoenix, a group of wizards fighting secretly against Voldemort. The Ministry's pigheaded outlook has disastrous consequences for Hogwarts, which buckles under Ministry decrees limiting freedom of speech, assembly, and information-prohibitions that hinder Harry, Ron, and Hermione's attempts to support the Order and repel Voldemort. Persecuted by the diabolical Dolores Umbridge, Ministry official and self-proclaimed deity, Harry forms an underground resistance, but even this triumph of wizard unity cannot dispel the uneasy mood as faithful teachers leave Hogwarts, and students such as Malfoy gain tremendous power. Now fifteen years old, Rowling's characters struggle to reveal themselves as adolescents, but these half-hearted attempts are soon overshadowed by the Herculean conflict facing them and by their immutable innocence, simply displayed in their direct opposition to a figure of pure evil.

Forced to wait for Voldemort's attack, Harry and the others exist in an ominous holding pattern, which draws the book inexorably to its deliciously tense finale. Superlative dialogue, suspenseful subplots, and Fred and George's brilliance balance the tone of despair, but the balance is at best a tenuous one. The climactic death of a main character and a horrifying revelation drag the book back into uncertainty and inaction in its concluding pages. As consolation, Rowling offers the unreserved love and loyalty of Harry's ever-growing "family," a force stronger even than Voldemort. Screaming with injustice and sorrow, this book's genius lies in its passion, which never falters. As does Professor McGonagall, readers find that the more Harry is disenfranchised, the greater is their determination to stand by him, to love him, and what he represents.—Caitlin Augusta."

_____. **The Tales of Beedle the Bard**. Scholastic, 2008. 128p. $12.99. 978-0-545-12828-5.
VOYA April 2009. **5Q · 5P · M · J · S** (SF/F/H)

Any question about Rowling's imagination and creativity is laid to rest with this book. The introduction is captivating, explaining that Beedle's tales are to wizard children what fairy tales are to muggles and that Professor Dumbledore had written commentary on them. The tales themselves are entertaining; with magical beings discovering that magic alone cannot solve one's problems. Dumbledore's commentary after each tale provides insight and history. In The Wizard and the Hopping Pot, the evil son of a kindly wizard inherits his father's magic pot, which the father used to help his muggle neighbors whenever asked. The son chooses to ignore his neighbors' misery, whereupon the pot tortures the son with noises and stench until he relents and helps his neighbors as did his father. Dumbledore's notes then explain that this tale was out of step with its time as it was written during a period of persecution of witches and wizards all over Europe. **The Tales of Beedle the Bard** appears as part of the final *Harry Potter* book with "The Tale of the Three Brothers" being featured. A passing knowledge of the Potter stories is helpful, but one need not have read all seven books to thoroughly enjoy Beedle. Rowling is at the top of her game as a superb storyteller, providing her legion of fans with an enchanting collection of wizard folklore.—Debbie Clifford.

Rubens, Michael. **Sons of the 613**. Clarion/Houghton Mifflin Harcourt, 2012. 320p. $16.99. 978-0-547-61216-4.
VOYA October 2012. **5Q · 5P · J · S**

This realistic fiction novel opens with the protagonist, Isaac, attending a Bar Mitzvah of one of his peers; however, this is no normal Bar Mitzvah. If you imagine the things that could go wrong in a Bar Mitzvah—they do. Eric Weinberg messed up big time as he read religious scripture in front of family and friends. Isaac becomes horrified after witnessing Eric's unfortunate spectacle. Isaac's Bar Mitzvah is in two weeks, and he feels unprepared. Even worse, his parents have to go to Italy for the next two weeks, so they ask his older, hotheaded brother, Josh, to take care of Isaac and his younger sister, Lisa. Soon, Josh turns this major responsibility into a quest. As Josh trains Isaac for his Bar Mitzvah, he puts his younger brother through emotional and physical trials. Isaac could probably rebel, but he chooses not to, for various reasons.

The Bar Mitzvah is a rite of passage in the Jewish religion. It is easy for young adults to identify with similar customs that prevail within different cultures and religions. This sexual-identity, coming-of-age, dark comedy could easily turn into a major motion picture. It is a novel for those twelve and up. The reader should have a box of tissue nearby for the conclusion.—Sharon Blumberg.

Rucker, Rudy. **Frek and the Elixir**. Tor, 2004. 476p. PLB $23.95. 978-1-4352-9197-3. $20.99 Trade pb. 978-0-7653-1059-0.
   VOYA October 2004. **5Q · 5P · J · S · A/YA** (SF/F/H)
   Rudy Rucker's **Frek and the Elixir** is a "wild and crazy" ride into the Toyland of "biotweaked critters" of 3003, where the government of NuBioCom has reduced Nature to only those items can be useful albeit marvelously "tweaked," and reduced human life to mechanized robots controlled by the Gov. When a spaceship lands in his room on an otherwise boring morning, young Frek Huggins is induced to leaved home to seek his runaway father who has resisted being "managed" by the pervasive Gov. As Frek begins his journey, find that does not know whom he can trust. His mother's instructions seem to betray him to the Gov. What he has always thought to be true seems false now.

   Frek's mythic adolescent odyssey to explore his roots and find his self is told with enchanting ingenuity that reflects the intellect of author Rucker, who has also written nonfiction about the fourth dimension of space as well as other well-received novels. On every page appears brilliantly conceived new creatures and situations—some elfin, some gross, and others just funny. Rucker's invented words seem exactly right both in sound and in sense. Every reader will be able to identify with the solidly normal Frek and his cohorts, but no reader could conceive of all the marvelously quirky details of this satisfying adventure—a wonderful surprise appears at each turn. Reminiscent of the Harry Potter series because of the traditional young adult plot, the changing relationships among the characters, and the continuously changing setting, this book beams with crazier, quicker humor. Accessible and suitable for young adult readers, it will also please those readers who consider themselves intelligently sophisticated—great science fiction!—Suzanne Elizabeth Reid.

Sanderson, Brandon. **Alcatraz Versus the Evil Librarians**. Scholastic, 2007. 320p. $16.99. 978-0-439-92550-1. PLB $15.99. 978-1-4395-8880-2. $6.99 pb. 978-0-439-92552-5.
   VOYA October 2007. **5Q · 5P · M · J**
   Alcatraz Smedry has a talent-for breaking things. It is not something that endears him to the foster parents to whom he has been assigned. On his thirteenth birthday, Alcatraz receives a box of sand and a note claiming that it is his inheritance. He then burns down the kitchen. Before he can be relocated, the box of sand is stolen, he is attacked by a gun-wielding stranger, and he is rescued by a man claiming to be his grandfather. It

turns out that Alcatraz is not living in the real world but trapped in the Hushlands, controlled by evil librarians feeding misinformation to an unsuspecting public. In a place where swords are more potent than guns, dinosaurs are proper English gentlemen, and only special glasses enable Alcatraz to see the truth, a talent for breaking things might be the only thing that can save the world.

In this original, hysterical homage to fantasy literature (Grandpa Smedry's exclamations such as "Edible Eddings!" are nods to masters of the genre), Sanderson's first novel for youth recalls the best in *Artemis Fowl* and *A Series of Unfortunate Events*. The humor, although broad enough to engage preteens, is also sneakily aimed at adults (there is a reason why the dinosaurs eat the "C" section in science fiction). "Authors," says Alcatraz, "write books for one, and only one, reason: because we like to torture people." Readers are indeed tortured, with quirky, seemingly incompetent heroes; dastardly villains fond of torture; cars that drive themselves; nonstop action; and cliffhanger chapter endings. And as soon as they finish the last wickedly clever page, they will be standing in line for more from this seasoned author of such adult-marketed titles as **Elantris** (Tor, 2005/**VOYA** October 2005).—Arlene Garcia.

Schmidt, Gary D. **What Came from the Stars**. Clarion/Houghton Mifflin Harcourt, 2012. 304p. $16.99. 978-0-547-61213-3.
   VOYA October 2012. **5Q 5P J**

Twelve-year-old Tommy Pepper is having a rough year. He endures not only nasty bullying by Cheryl Lumpkin, but threats from Cheryl's politically powerful, realtor mother who wants the Pepper's ramshackle Plymouth, MA, oceanfront home demolished to make way for an exclusive development. He is traumatized by his belief that his beloved mother's death on an icy road months earlier was his fault. At the same time, on a far-off planet, the peaceful Valorim are being annihilated by Lord Mondus and the O'Mondim. In the face of a fierce battle, Young Waeglim is determined to save his people and their precious Art of Valorim, a magical chain of power. He hurls it through the cosmos and it lands in Tommy Pepper's Ace Robotroid Adventure lunchbox. Tommy slips the chain around his neck and absorbs the language, knowledge, and courage of the Valorim. Soon, Tommy is matching wits on two increasingly dangerous fronts—an infiltrator from the Lord Mondus camp is hired as a teacher at Tommy's school, and the residents of Plymouth are under attack as well.

Award-winning author Schmidt (Newbery, National Book Award finalist, and Printz Honor) is a wondrous writer. He beautifully blends ferocious battle scenes on a far-off planet with the tender struggles of Tommy's grief, familial devotion, and suffering from bullying, even as his emerging confidence and courage draw him into the Valorim/O'Mondim fray. Add in perfectly placed moments of sweet humor to relieve the tension, and Schmidt delivers a wonderful story that will have more than one reader going back to the beginning to pick up clues missed in the first go-round. A glossary of his Schmidt's inventive Valorim language is a plus.—Beth E. Andersen.

Scott, Kieran. **He's So Not Worth It**. Simon & Schuster, 2011. 368p. $16.99. 978-1-4169-9953-9.

    VOYA June 2011. **5Q · 5P · J · S**

Ally Ryan and her parents left Orchard Hill after her dad lost most of their money, as well as the money of their friends and neighbors. Ally and her mom moved back last year, to the poor side of town, and Ally has done her best to make a new life. Jake, the boy living in her old house and tight with her old friends, might be the best part. Or it seems that way, until Jake lets Ally's ex-best friend humiliate her in public. But Jake will be able to make it up to Ally over the summer, right? Wrong. Ally is off to the Jersey Shore and Jake is stuck at home with a job and school work. When Jake hears Ally is dating, he makes some bad choices with lasting consequences. Truthfully, Ally's choices are not that much better. Can the pair turn things around for a happy ending?

Readers looking for something with just the right blend of old-fashioned angst, tangled relationships, and romantic troubles for the teens and their parents, will do cartwheels while enjoying every page of this book. As the second in a trilogy, this could have easily become a placeholder, but instead delivers its own intricate storyline while nicely advancing the overarching plot started in **She's So Dead to Us** (Simon & Schuster, 2010). Not a cautionary tale, but realistically adding underage drinking and evidence of sexual activity help to create another layer of drama. The repercussions, both large and small, are hinted at but not fully revealed making for a slam-dunk, cliffhanger ending.—Stacey Hayman.

_____. **This Is So Not Happening: He's So/She's So**. Simon & Schuster, 2012. 320p. $16.99. 978-1-4169-9955-3.

    VOYA April 2012. **5Q · 5P · S**

Ally and Jake are looking forward to starting their senior year at Orchard Hill High as a happy couple, but considering their past, they should buckle up for a bumpy ride. The bump turns out to be a baby bump. When their mutual friend Chloe, the soon-to-be mom, names Jake as the father, he believes it is possible. Ally wants to stand by her man and Jake wants to step-up for Chloe, but can they do it? Jake's grades suffer and finding a balance between almost-dad vs. boyfriend seems impossible. Ally is dealing with her Mom's upcoming second marriage and supporting the teen parents, but feeling understandably hurt as Jake begins to focus more on Chloe. When doubt is cast on the baby's paternity and Jake refuses to question what he has been told, the truth of this complicated situation takes them for a ride.

Oh the drama! Oh the half-truths and outright lies! This story is equal parts juicy teen soap and thought-provoking, discussable novel for all ages. A well-rounded group of friends and family are in the background of this story, and their presence is notable even though Jake and Ally are the only narrators. Understanding the thought processes, explaining the reason behind a choice, and feeling the positive/negative reactions of those closest to the situation allow readers to truly appreciate the outcome. Fans of MTV's 16 and Pregnant and Teen Mom will find this book particularly fascinating, but it will equally appeal to anyone who enjoys a love story with plenty of ups and downs, interesting characters, and a satisfying ending. This is a great conclusion to an engaging series.—Stacey Hayman.

Sheinkin, Steve. **Bomb: The Race to Build—and Steal—the World's Most Dangerous Weapon**. Flash Point/Macmillan, 2012. 272p. $19.99. 978-1-59643-487-5. Photos. Notes. Index.
VOYA October 2012. **5Q · 5P · M · J · S · A/YA** (NF)
Excellence in Nonfiction for Young Adults 2013

Sheinkin skillfully piques the interest of readers, from pre-teen through adult, by combining all the pieces of the puzzle leading up to the development and implementation of the nuclear weapons used by the United States against Japan in 1945. He brings the story to life by introducing a varied cast of characters along the way. The spies, inventors, physicists, code breakers, laboratory workers, resistance fighters, and political leaders involved in the race for the ultimate weapon and the climactic end of World War II are presented in relatable terms. The story opens with a little known character, Harry Gold, as he is about to be apprehended by the FBI after years of investigation for espionage. The scene is set for the back story of all the other figures in the complex history of the project. Readers become informed participant observers along the way. There is just enough science in the book to educate the reader about atomic energy without overwhelming those not scientifically inclined.

The photographs, notes and index are outstanding. This well-paced and very human story reminds the reader of the long-range impact of the bomb on the generations after the first use warfare. Readers are also reminded of the continuing concerns about the use of nuclear energy. "One of history's most amazing examples of teamwork and genius and poise under pressure" is also a caveat for our children: "It's a story with no end in sight. And like it or not, you're in it." Sheinkin's previous book, **The Notorious Benedict Arnold**, won numerous awards, and this work is bound to join those illustrious ranks. It combines elements of a gripping suspense thriller with the plain truth and realism of its subject, ever reminding us of the "story" within history. This title is highly recommended for all public libraries, as well as academic collections.—Jane Murphy.

Silvey, Anita. **Everything I Need to Know I Learned from a Children's Book**. Roaring Brook/Macmillan, 2009. 233p. $29.99. 978-1-59643-395-3. Index. Illus. Biblio.
VOYA February 2010. **5Q · 5P · S · A/YA**

"Everything is interesting if you stop and look at it." That observation by the writer David Macaulay is an apt summation for this compendium of classic children's literature. Award-winning educator Silvey compiles more than one hundred essays of varying lengths by celebrities, writers, illustrators, academics, business leaders, and athletes. Each contributor—from writer Sherman Alexie to First Book founder Kyle Zimmer—discusses one children's book that made a difference in his or her world. An excerpt from the cited title accompanies each essay along with its original artwork and includes captivating publication facts and a brief author biography. Endnotes provide an extensive list of recommended children's books divided by age and genre, selected titles written by the contributors, and further biographical information.

Everyone who loves children's literature will relish this beautiful book. It offers a terrific opportunity to mine the depths of children's publishing, mostly from the early to mid-twentieth century. The usual suspects are well represented—**Huckleberry Finn**, for example, and **Little House on the Prairie** get their deserved praise—but the true gems are the out-of-print titles that illuminate the timeless qualities of being a child. Readers will delight in memories, for example, of **Miss Pickerell Goes to Mars** by Ellen MacGregor (1951) or **Poppy Ott and the Galloping Snail** by Leo Edwards (1927). Mostly, however, readers will savor the loving tone of these diverse and honest narratives. It is an essential purchase for nonfiction collections.—Christina Fairman.

Simmons, Michael. **Finding Lubchenko**. Razorbill/Penguin, 2005. 288p. $16.99. 978-1-59514-021-0.
VOYA June 2005. **5Q · 5P · J · S**
Popular Paperbacks for Young Adults 2009.

Genius, underachieving, delinquent 16-year-old Evan Macalister combats biological terrorism, saves his father from a murder frame-up and gets the girl in this hilarious mystery framed in generational conflict. Evan's 70-year-old, emotionally distant, multimillionaire father wants Evan to learn the value of a dollar and star academically. Evan, who reads people rather than books, steals equipment from his father's medical company, which has a biological weapon division, and earns D and F grades as well as discipline referrals at his uptight private school. When Evan's father is arrested for straggling an employee whose laptop Evan has stolen, Rueben, Evan's unwilling partner in crime, breaks the computer's codes and discovers the name of the murdered man's Paris contact. Reuben, Evan, and Evan's love interest, who speaks perfect French, travel first class to Paris to meet Lubchenko. Distracted by Paris nightlife, they find Lubchenko, who fingers the culprit, reveals plans to sell a smallpox virus, and gives Evan information to clear his father. But they must get that information to the proper authorities without getting killed or revealing their source.

As with Simmons's **Pool Boy** (Roaring Brook, 2003/**VOYA** June 2003), this coming of age story features a lovable anti-hero telling his story in a sarcastic insightful voice. It also shares a father in jail, a stabilizing parent figure outside the family, and a seemingly impossible love interest. Because Evan keeps his underground activities secret, it could produce many entertaining teenage detective/spy sequels.—Lucy Schall.

Slater, Adam. **The Shadowing: Hunted**. Egmont, 2011. 208p. $16.99. 978-1-60684-261-4.
VOYA October 2011. **5Q · 5P · M · J · S**

Callum has always been able to see ghosts, but what used to be occasional sightings are becoming constant. He also has what he refers to as "the Luck," a sixth sense that warns him about trouble. Coming home one night, he feels as though he is being watched, hunted. He dreams that night of a gruesome murder of a teenaged boy and learns the next morning that it had happened. Thanks to a premonition, he saves a classmate, Melissa, from a bully's prank that would have been fatal. Melissa is a New Age, crystal–wearing believer in things that cannot be seen. She quickly realizes that Callum has abilities. Feeling accepted, he tells her about the dreams and about seeing the spirit of a large black dog and a teenaged boy in the graveyard of a nearby church. She tells him it is a "churchyard Grim" and encourages him to investigate further with her help. She becomes a translator between Callum, the Grim, and his master, Jacob, who informs Callum that he is a chime child, and that his growing abilities are to prepare him to fight in the upcoming Shadowing, when the boundaries of the mortal world and the netherworld are weakened. His abilities also have put him in danger from the Hunter who feeds on chime children.

There is almost nonstop action from the first page and the tension builds steadily to the last. Fans of the paranormal will scoop this up and be clamoring for the sequel, including the most reluctant readers.—Suanne Roush.

Smith, Alexander Gordon. **Death Sentence: Escape from Furnace 3**. Farrar, Straus, Giroux/Macmillan, 2011. 272p. $15.99. 978-0-374-32494-0.
VOYA June 2011. **5Q · 5P · J · S**
Quick Picks for Reluctant Young Readers 2012.

The Black Coats have captured Alex. His second attempt at escape has failed, and now his demise is imminent. Inmates who are caught by the Black Coats do not return—at least not in their normal guise. They are transformed into beasts, ruthless monsters that possess no reason at all. If Alex is lucky enough to survive the nectar and surgical procedures, he will become one of them as well; the hunted will become the hunter. Alex will discover the horrific truth behind Furnace and will be forced to fight to maintain his own humanity. All he has to do is remember his name—such a simple thing, but perhaps too difficult for even Alex to accomplish.

In this third installment of the Furnace series, Gordon-Smith has pulled out all the stops. It is a tour de force of action and adventure. The novel opens with Alex uttering the line, "I died in that room." And, in fact, it is true—Alex dies and is reborn a monster. The novel centers on Alex and his humanity. But is Alex strong enough to hang on to it, or will he become another mindless pawn in Alfred Furnace's sick game? Honestly, this reviewer could not put this book down, having thoroughly enjoyed all of the novels in this series, and will anxiously await the release of Fugitives: Escape from Furnace 4 due winter 2012. Please continue to wow us, Mr. Gordon Smith—your books are a pleasure to read.—Jonatha Basye.

Snicket, Lemony. **"Who Could That Be at This Hour?" All the Wrong Questions**. Illus. by Seth. Little, Brown, 2012. 272p. $15.99. 978-0-316-12308-2.
VOYA December 2012. **5Q · 5P · M**

In this first entry of his new series, *All the Wrong Questions*, Lemony Snicket turns the lens on himself, describing his apprenticeship with a secret organization at age thirteen. Young Lemony has just finished his unusual education and has begun his first assignment in the town of Stain'd-by-the-Sea. He and his chaperone have been hired to track down a stolen statue of great value. When they find the statue, they discover it has not been stolen and has no value, except, seemingly, to the criminal Hangfire. The book ends with no resolution to the case. Secondary plot lines concern Lemony's place within the organization, a self-appointed task to tunnel under a museum, and his relationship with an "associate" who turns out to be his sister.

Fans of *A Series of Unfortunate Events* will recognize elements of the previous stories (the V.F.D., certain characters), but readers not familiar with Snicket's earlier work will still find much to enjoy. This book is full of Snicket's characteristic wit and word play. Stain'd-by-the-Sea is populated with quirky characters, from the reporter, Moxie Mallahan, to Pip and Squeak, two young taxi drivers, who fit seamlessly into the world Snicket has created. Seth's two-color, black-and-blue illustrations fit the mood of the book perfectly, and provide additional information to the story, particularly concerning secondary plot lines. This book belongs in all collections serving middle school students. Readers will be eagerly awaiting the next volume in the series.—Bethany Martin.

Spotswood, Jessica. **Born Wicked: The Cahill Witch Chronicles, Book One**. Putnam/Penguin, 2012. 272p. $17.99. 978-0-399-25745-2.
VOYA April 2012. **5Q · 5P · J · S**

In New England during the late 1890s, at a place and time where witches are condemned, Cate Cahill and her two younger sisters must hide their true identity. Being discovered by the Brotherhood could bring about an early end to their young lives. Before the death of their mother, Cate made a promise to protect her sisters. With only six months before having to choose between marriage and the Sisterhood, keeping her word proves harder than she has imagined. To make matters worse, she discovers her mother's diary, which reveals a devastating secret that could potentially destroy her family. Desperate to find another way, Cate seeks help from old acquaintances and new friends. At the same time, she manages to balance social gatherings, marriage proposals, and a forbidden romance.

Spotwood's debut novel is enchanting and addicting. **Born Wicked** is a beautiful beginning to *The Cahill Witch Chronicles*. The author's elegant writing supports a well-constructed plot and realistic characters. The story provides an alternative history that draws from the Salem witch trials and Puritanism. The Brotherhood upholds the laws by keeping a watchful eye on the members of society. The dynamic characters bring the suspenseful story to life. The Cahill sisters are a feisty, rebellious trio that readers will not forget. This paranormal romance will capture any reader's imagination, even if he or she is not interested in witchcraft and magic. It is a must-have for any library.—Lindsey Weaver.

Stahl, R. James. **Merlyn's Pen: Fiction, Essays, and Poems by American Teens, Volume IV**. Merlyn's Pen, 2001. 99p. Trade pb. 978-1-886427-50-1. O.P. Index. Illus. Photos.
VOYA August 2001. **5Q · 5P · M · J · S** (NF)

Teachers looking for examples of student writing for their own teens to read and model will want to seek out this exemplary tool. The annual publication's mission statement is clearly defined and followed as it "seeks to broaden and reward the young author's interest in writing, strengthen the self-confidence of beginning writers, and promote among all students a positive attitude toward literature." Each writer included in the collection is an American middle school or high school teen writing messages and stories of young adult interest. The genres represented include fiction, short stories, essays, memoirs, and poetry. An added bonus is the bio of each author, which provides the reader with insight into the writing lives of published teens. Each selection is cross-referenced by theme and grade level, which will help teachers meet their students' needs. The content of the high school selections is appropriate for younger readers, so teachers need not concern themselves with censoring the language or topics to which younger readers might be introduced. Older readers will find stories and poems that speak to them in their own language on topics including abuse, love, loss, family, friendships, and coming of age.

This text meets the needs of teachers and students in the reading or writing classroom. Readers will find engaging stories and poems with which they can identify, and teachers will have a useful teaching tool conveniently available.—Denise Beasely.

Stewart, Jon, with The Daily Show Staff. **The Daily Show with Jon Stewart Presents America (The Book): A Citizen's Guide to Democracy Inaction**. Warner, 2004. 221p. $15.99 Trade pb. 978-0-446-69186-4. Illus. Photos. Maps. Charts. **VOYA** April 2005. **5Q · 5P · S · A/YA** (NF)

Starting with a stamped "This book is the property of . . ." form in the inside front cover to a "Certificate of Completion" stating that the "student" is "thus fully qualified to practice, participate in, or found a democracy," this book is everything that an ordinary U.S. history textbook is not. After a satirical foreword by Thomas Jefferson-"but I digress. My point in composing the Declaration of Independence and the Constitution was hard work. God didn't dictate it for us to transcribe. . . . We created a blueprint for a system that would endure, which means your lazy asses shouldn't be coasting on our accomplishments."-the book's ten memorable chapters include "Democracy Before America," "The Founding of America," "The President: King of Democracy," "Congress: Quagmire of Freedom," "The Judicial Branch: It Rules," "Campaigns and Elections: America Changes the Sheets," "The Media: Democracy's Valiant Vulgarians," "The Future of Democracy: Four Score and Seven Years from Now," and "The Rest of the World: International House of Horrors." Plenty of photos and factoids as sidebars such as "Were You Aware? Plato did not originally want to call the Athenian form of citizen-government, 'Democracy," but rather, 'Plato 'n Friends.'" Or "Fun Fact: Jesus lived to be 33, one fewer than the number of home runs Boog Powell hit in 1966!" There are equally wonderful cross-sections of the president's house, the campaign bus, a poster on "the shadow government," and a map of the future Washington, D.C. The visuals complement the text perfectly in full color and with zany labels. Both parties, all parts of the government, the election process, the media, and just about everything else political in the nation is up for satiric grabs, but the overall effect is to highlight the careless ways in which the nation practices democracy and to make readers think.

This satire on American history textbooks by the host and staff of The Daily Show, possibly the only funny thing to come out of the recent election, is totally hilarious in exactly the irreverent way that bright teenagers will love. Everybody gets hit, not the least of whom are Supreme Court justices, whose faces atop naked, age-appropriate bodies appear with tabbed black robes to play judicial paper dolls, which got the book banned in Wal Mart and will no doubt arouse (pun intended) the ire of humorless censors everywhere. Resist them, and make sure that the best local social studies teachers have copies. One cannot imagine smart teens not loving this book.—Mary K. Chelton.

Stiefvater, Maggie. **Linger**. *Wolves of Mercy Falls*. Scholastic, 2010. 368p. $17.99. 978-0-545-12328-0.
VOYA August 2010. **5Q · 5P · J ·** (SF/F/H)

In **Shiver** (Scholastic, 2009/**VOYA** December 2009), Grace watched Sam struggle to remain human instead of succumbing to the call of the wild, brought on by the bitter Minnesota cold. In this sequel, Sam, now human, watches Grace, the only victim of a werewolf attack who didn't turn, go through the same struggle as her body demands that she take the form of a wolf. Used to the benign neglect of parents too busy with their own lives to pay attention to their teenage daughter, Grace has Sam sharing her bedroom, until her parents intervene at the worst possible time, when Grace is losing her battle with the turn and needs Sam more than ever. Against this intense Romeo and Juliet scenario another pair of lovers serves as counterpoint. Cole, a famous Indie rock star sees becoming a wolf as the ultimate escape, even better than drugs. Only his body is not reacting the way it should, and he is spending too much time in human form, haunted by the personal demons of his past and the beginnings of a very strange relationship with Isabel. Viciously intelligent, sharp and biting at her best, Isabelle saw her brother die trying to reclaim his humanity and now fights her attraction to a boy deliberately trying to lose his.

This riveting narrative, impossible to put down, is not only an excellent addition to the current fangs and fur craze but is also a beautifully written romance that, along with **Shiver**, will have teens clamoring for the third and final entry.—Bonnie Kunzel.

_____. **Shiver**. *Wolves of Mercy Falls*. Scholastic, 2009. 400p. $17.99. 978-0-545-12326-6. $8.99 pb. 978-0-545-12327-3.
VOYA December 2009. **5Q · 5P · J · S** (SF/F/H)
Best Books for Young Adults 2010.
Quick Picks for Reluctant Young Readers 2010.
Popular Paperbacks for Young Adutls 2011
Teens' Top Ten 2010.

Grace and Sam met six years ago when she was attacked by werewolves. Sam changed from a yellow-eyed wolf to a yellow-eyed boy and carried her home. Although bitten, Grace survived and did not change, the only werewolf victim ever to do so. She has a more developed sense of smell, improved hearing, is stronger physically, but she is still a girl, only now a girl connected to a wolf, her guardian who watches her every winter. When Grace finally meets Sam again in human form, it is in the fall of her seventeenth year. Sam, attacked and forcibly changed when he was seven, has grown up spending his winters with Beck, his werewolf mentor, running through the woods with the pack, and his summers in human form, learning how to read, write, and become a man. The chapters have temperatures for headings because these werewolves are turned, not by a full moon, but by the cold, and there is plenty of cold in Mercy Falls, Minnesota. Also the number of times they can change is limited, and this change may be Sam's last in human form. After the wolves attack a local teenager, Sam is shot and winds up in Grace's arms, literally. She saves him, but the days are getting colder and the nights longer. Neither can bear the thought of being separated, but one cannot argue with Mother Nature.

The first volume in *The Wolves of Mercy Falls* series is yet another winner for the author of **Lament** (Flux/Llewellyn, 2008/**VOYA** December 2008). This novel is perfect for *Twilight* fans or a Romeo and Juliet list. It is sensuous, intense, riveting, and so very satisfying.—Bonnie Kunzel.

Stork, Francisco X. **Marcelo in the Real World**. Arthur A. Levine/Scholastic, 2009. 320p. $17.99. 978-0-545-05474-4. $8.99 Trade pb. 978-0-545-05690-8.
    VOYA June 2009. **5Q · 5P · S**
Top Ten Best Books for Young Adults 2010.

Marcelo—a teen who exhibits Asperger-like behaviors, including hearing a type of music no one else can—is offered an ultimatum by his father: unless Marcelo can successfully complete a summer job as a mail room clerk in his father's law firm, he have to attend a "regular" high school for his senior year instead of the specialized school he has attended for his entire academic career. It would mean giving up his cherished position as a stable boy working with Haflinger ponies and facing his reservations about the "real world." In the mailroom, Marcelo becomes involved in a mystery, which requires him to push his skills to a new level and make decisions about his beliefs, his family, and his future.

Marcelo is a believable character in a situation with which teens can empathize. The narrative is consistent and caringly crafted, offering a compelling examination of Marcelo's challenges and successes. Because many of the character interactions center on feelings and Marcelo's social growth, it would have been easy for the conversations to become didactic or over-the-top, but the author is able to keep the text focused and carry the story well. The nicely balanced mystery elements add texture to the plot and will keep readers engaged, and well-built secondary characters help the story feel complete. This beautifully written, insightful book is sure to resonate with many readers facing their own version of the real world, and belongs in all collections serving young adults and those who work with them.—Elsworth Rockefeller.

Stroud, Jonathan. **The Amulet of Samarkand**. *The Bartimaeus Trilogy*. Hyperion, 2003. 544p. $17.95. 978-0-7868-1859-4. $8.99 Trade pb. 978-0-7868-5255-0.
    VOYA December 2003. **5Q · 5P · M · J · S ·** (SF/F/H)
    Top Ten Best Books for Young Adults 2004.

When Nathaniel, an underestimated almost twelve-year-old boy magician, summons a centuries-old djinni named Bartimaeus, readers are off on a wild adventure with more narrow escapes than even Houdini could muster. Nathaniel is an apprentice to a master who bothers little with his training, so Mr. Underwood has no idea what Nathaniel's self-taught magical capabilities really are. Nathaniel's first task for the djinni startles even Bartimaeus, who has seen a lot in his day, as he wryly reminds readers throughout the novel. He charges Bartimaeus to steal the Amulet of Samarkand from Simon Lovelace as a matter of revenge for humiliating him while his master did nothing.

The escalating chain of events resulting from this theft is told in alternating viewpoints from Nathaniel and Bartimaeus, who uses sardonic footnotes to enhance his storytelling. The narrative also successfully uses both first and third person, a rich vocabulary, sophisticated wit, and a hierarchy of magical creatures woven into a fascinating plot that will be appreciated by fans of Diana Wynne Jones and other complex fantasy writers. Teens will race to the end to see if Nathaniel and Bartimaeus can work together to save London's magical community from Simon's evil plans. They will eagerly await the second book in this planned trilogy with a Miramax movie in the making. Fortunately, the quality is as high as the hype, but as Bartimaeus says in one of his footnotes, "Well, what are you hanging around reading this for? Read on quickly and see for yourself."-Cindy Dobrez.

_____. **Heroes of the Valley**. Hyperion/DBG, 2009. 480p. $17.99. 978-1-4231-0966-2. $8.99 pb. 978-1-4231-0967-9.
VOYA February 2009. **5Q · 5P · M · J** (SF/F/H)
Best Book for Young Adults 2010.

Stroud creates a credible and fully realized medieval setting for his protagonist, a hot-headed, short-limbed youth in need of proving himself against both mortal and immortal antagonists. Fifteen-year-old Halli Sveinsson, the second (and therefore superfluous) son of the house, has been reared on the tales of the heroes who settled the valley, ancestors who pounded out civility from feuding clans. When Halli's own words help to reignite a feud, he battles a brave young woman at his side against another heroic clan but also against the Trows, the mythic beasts that guard the valley, keeping the mortals in as much as their enemies out.

With perfect pacing, excellent character development of both Halli and the girl Aud, and suspense built as much of legends as of fantasy, there is high appeal here for both boys and girls—and, doubtless, for movie makers to come. Halli is a genuine hero, flawed as well as brave.—Francisca Goldsmith.

Van de Ruit, John. **Spud**. Razorbill/Penguin, 2007. 339p. PLB $18.99. 978-1-4395-9067-6. $9.99 Trade pb. 978-1-59514-187-3.
VOYA December 2007. **5Q · 5P · J · S**
Popular Paperbacks 2013.

South Africa, 1990-Mandela is released from prison, apartheid is abolished, and naïve John Milton, soon to be known as Spud, begins his scholarship year at a boys-only boarding school. A young-looking thirteen-year-old with a beautiful voice, John is placed in the treble, also called the "Spud," section. All the usual boarding-school pranks, anatomy references, and eccentric personalities are included in Spud's entertaining and lengthy diary. Finding his niche at school, coping with a hilariously dysfunctional family, and experiencing first love (more than once) comprise Spud's memorable year. Starring in the school's production of Oliver, he becomes the center of attention and unexpectedly popular with girls. Spud's diary is fresh and insightful, and some situations, especially those featuring his family, are laugh-out-loud funny.

The author creates a sympathetic, likeable character-the reader cheers for Spud all the way. With his embarrassing parents, eccentric grandmother, and unusual roommate who has the "nasty habit of pulling out large clumps of his own hair with a thunk," Spud's life never lacks drama or humor. More Adrian Mole (despite Spud's statement that "Adrian Mole wouldn't last one day in our dormitory") than Holden Caulfield, Spud appeals to a wide range of readers. Great literature? Maybe not. Great fun? Definitely. The deft blend of humor and seriousness makes a welcome addition to the coming-of-age genre, and the diary format engages the reader from the start. New fans will look forward to the sequel, **Spud: The Madness Continues** (Razorbill, 2008).—Judy Sasges.

Volponi, Paul. **Rucker Park Setup**. Viking, 2007. 153p. $15.99. 978-0-670-06130-3. $6.99 Trade pb. 978-0-14-241207-7.
VOYA June 2007. **5Q · 5P · M · J · S**
Quick Picks for Reluctant Young Adult Readers 2008.

J.R. and Mackey grew up playing pickup basketball in Harlem, and by the time they reached high school, there was no doubt that "these two got man-style game." Although the duo took Washington High to the state playoffs, garnered All City honors, and received college scholarship offers, their lifetime goal has always been winning the tournament at Rucker Park, the toughest, most prestigious basketball tournament in street ball. When their dream is on the verge of becoming reality, however, everything goes wrong. J.R. is murdered right on the court, and Mackey is left to clean up the mess that he may very well be responsible for creating. By the time the final whistle blows, Mackey will have to settle the score in both the game and the murder of his best friend.

The reader will have no doubt that Volponi has played street ball in New York City. His description of playing pickup ball on one of the toughest courts in the world feels wholly authentic. The characters also feel real and are probably composites of people Volponi has known. Readers need not be sports fans to enjoy the story; it has equal merit as a character study and has a surprising murder-mystery element as well. Language and violence do not rise to a level that would preclude middle school students from reading this book, and high school students will find the story and characterization complex enough to be an engaging read.—James Blasingame.

Wallace, Jason. **Out of Shadows**. Holiday House, 2011. 282p. $17.95. 978-0-8234-2342-2.
VOYA August 2011. **5Q · 5P · M · J · A/YA**
Best Fiction for Young Adults 2012.

Racial tensions are simmering as thirteen-year-old Robert Jacklin arrives at a prestigious boarding school in Zimbabwe in the 1980s. Robert, who is white and misses his mother, immediately declares brotherhood with his roommate, Nelson, who is black, but soon finds himself drawn to racist bully Ivan. Spurred by a charismatic teacher, Ivan and his friends, fueled with hatred for controversial Zimbabwe president Robert Mugabe and the ruling party, begin to take a dark path tormenting the local youth, and Robert soon wonders if he has gotten in over his head.

Wallace's book is devastatingly stunning, inviting comparisons with Bryce Courtenay's **The Power of One** (Ballantine, 1990/**VOYA** December 1989), if the hero of that novel aligned himself with the bad guys. Drawing on memories of his own experiences in a Zimbabwe boarding school, Wallace does not shy away from portraying his characters realistically and unflatteringly. Even Jacklin is not blameless, which makes it all the more powerful when he sees what his own actions have wrought. The author explains why Ivan is so terrible, and while we never root for him, we see where he is coming from and recognize our own potential slippery slopes. The book never fades or lets up, even when it threatens to boil over into a political thriller. It is an unflinching look at hatred and the human damage it leaves in its wake.—Matthew Weaver.

Werlin, Nancy. **The Rules of Survival**. Dial, 2006. 272p. $17.99. 978-0-8037-3001-4. $7.99 Trade pb. 978-0-14-241071-4.
VOYA October 2006. **5Q · 5P · S**
Top Ten Best Books for Young Adults 2007.
Populat Paperbacks for Young Adutls 2010.
Quick Picks for for Reluctant Young Adult Readers 2007.

Unlike Werlin's previous four novels, this latest includes nary a mystery element. But the departure from genre does not mean that Werlin's newest book lacks suspense. If anything, it is one of her most deliciously harrowing works. Eighteen-year-old narrator Matthew introduces the novel with a letter to his younger sister, Emmy; the body of the book is what he calls the "true story of our family's past" and is written in short, tight, first-person chapters that occasionally address his sister-and readers, his "real" audience. In the novel, Matthew recounts his thirteenth through sixteenth years, during which he, Emmy, and their "middle" sister, Callie, lived in a small apartment in South Boston with their manic and abusive mother. Much of what Matthew describes involves his and Callie's attempts to protect the younger and more vulnerable Emmy. The siblings spend much of their time on edge, attempting to appease their mercurial mother and protect Emmy from her often-violent wrath. When their mother begins dating a complicated man named Murdoch, Matthew casts this newcomer as the family's savior and is frustrated and depressed when Murdoch does not immediately rise to the occasion.

The plot moves swiftly and unrelentingly to a climax that visits themes common to some of Werlin's earlier works and offers an uneasy recognition of the same conclusion David Yaffe voiced in **The Killer's Cousin** (Delacorte, 1998/**VOYA** October 1998), "Anyone in this world can have the power of life and death over someone else. It's horrible, but true."-Amy S. Pattee.

Whelan, Gloria. **Homeless Bird**. HarperCollins, 2000. 192p. PLB $14.99. 978-1-4352-6393-2. $5.99 Trade pb. 978-0-06-440819-6. Glossary.
VOYA February 2001. **5Q · 5P · J · S**
Top Ten Best Books for Young Adults 2001.
Popular Paperbacks for Young Adults 2002.
National Book Award for Young People's Literature 2000.

Thirteen-year-old Koly is from a poor family in India. She enters into an arranged marriage with a sixteen-year-old boy, only to discover that her new husband is very ill. The only reason his parents wanted him to marry Koly was to get their hands on her dowry to finance a trip to find a cure for their son. When her young husband dies, Koly is left under the supervision of her dreadful mother-in-law. When Koly's supportive father-in-law also dies, her mother-in-law abandons Koly in the city. Koly must find her way on her own. As she does, she encounters help from strangers, including a handsome young man, but she also relies on her own inner resources and talents.

Homeless Bird has all the elements of a great read-a strong, empathetic heroine, a fascinating culture, triumph over adversity, conflict between tradition and modern-day needs and wants, romance, and hope for the future. The story is beautifully written, weaving in Hindi words that are defined in the glossary provided in the back of the book. Despite the obvious elements of fairy tale-cruel mother-in-law, attractive young male coming to the rescue-the book does not slide into cliché but is unsentimental and fresh. Homeless Bird will satisfy many readers and belongs in every school and public library collection.—Alice Stern.

White, Kiersten. **Endlessly: Paranormalcy**. HarperCollins, 2012. 400p. $17.99. 978-0-06-198588-1.
VOYA April 2012. **5Q · 5P · J · S**

Despite the growing assortment of paranormals in her small Virginia town, Evie is happy to focus on the upcoming winter formal and spending time with her boyfriend, Lend, but normal for Evie does not seem to last long. A coalition of known and new-to-Evie paranormals is waiting to ask a final favor: will she make a gate that will return them to their world before they are trapped here forever? Struggling against rival Faerie Court forces, an out-of-control IPCA, and her own uncertainty about which choice is right, Evie needs to decide soon. Is she willing to try and if she does, would her effort be in time?

Readers thinking they are about to sit back and relax with the third and final installment in the *Paranormalcy* series should think again. Tension begins building soon after the story starts and continues to grow through one dramatic, dangerous episode after another, with no relief in sight. Fans who love Evie's signature style of butt-kicking, wise-cracking, headlong rushing into trouble, neatly mixed with her addiction to all things romantic and girly, will embrace every nerve-wracking moment. There is plenty of substance beneath all the style too, with thoughtful explanations of complex questions which have plagued readers from the start. Key characters, past and present, receive attention and satisfying send-offs, allowing teens to imagine a future for them all.

The challenge of making this book stand on its own, while concluding the series, was more than met by the author. It is a sparkly gift tied-up with a pretty pink bow, and readers everywhere will say, "Thank you!"—Stacey Hayman.

Wolf, Elaine. **Camp**. Sky Pony, 2012. 256p. $16.95. 978-1-61608-657-2.
VOYA December 2012. **5Q · 5P · J · S**

Amy Becker is fourteen, lonely, and troubled, stuck in her own angst evolving from rejecting her über-controlling, German-immigrant mother and caring for her autistic brother, Charlie. Her dad struggles to keep the peace, but Amy wishes her strict, demanding mother were dead. Then, Uncle Ed buys a summer camp in Maine, and Amy reluctantly heads for the wilderness, where she finds her fellow campers far more deceiving than her secretive mother. Amy's chief nemesis is Rory, a troubled deviant whose goal is to bully Amy into silence about the cruel mistreatment she and her pals create. Erin befriends Amy, and for once she has a true confidante and comrade.

Wolf is known as a champion anti-bullying advocate, but there is much more to this story than applauding Amy's efforts in learning to stand up for herself. Secrets meander through the pages and threaten to tear Amy's world apart. The tension mounts as readers wonder why Amy cannot bring herself to reveal the torture she is undergoing at camp, what Amy's mother is hiding, or what will happen when the truth prevails. The story is set in 1963; the timeframe contributes to the climax, but the awful price Amy must pay in her coming-of-age story resonates with horror and redemption as the denouement leaves the reader breathless. This mesmerizing book is a must-read for adolescents and the adults who care about them.—Judith A. Hayn.

Wolfson, Jill. **What I Call Life**. Henry Holt & Company, 2005. 272p. $16.95. 978-0-8050-7669-1. $6.99 Trade pb. 978-0-312-37752-6.
VOYA December 2005. **5Q · 5P · M · J**

Eleven-year-old Cal Lavender is used to trouble. She blames herself when her mother explodes at the library and they are ushered out by police—Betty to God knows where, and Cal to the foster home called "Pumpkin House." Cal assumes her Face for Unbearably Unpleasant and Embarrassing Situations and prepares to cope, which she does very well; Cal is always in control. Her housemates are special; Amber does not speak, Fern laughs constantly, Monica has a broken arm, and Whitney was born with a defective heart and has become a veteran of so many foster homes that she has lost count. Knitting Lady, their ancient caregiver, entertains them with serial stories about a foster girl. As she teaches them to knit and to understand their feelings, they learn that "different" does not mean "bad," and that imperfect parents can be forgiven. When Betty returns at last, Cal's life does not become typical, and that is just fine. As the Knitting Lady says, "Everyone is always living her story."

Wolfson's first novel is a grand-slam homerun. Her wonderfully kooky characters; her fast-paced, witty dialogue; and her realistic depiction of emotional growth in severely damaged children keep the reader laughing and crying on every page. In the fine tradition of Haulden Caulfield and Huckleberry Finn, Cal is lovable unforgettable.

Somewhere, perhaps inside of every reader, is a child who will be reaffirmed by this exceptional piece of middle school fiction.—Laura Woodruff.

Wrede, Patricia C., and Caroline Stevermer. **Sorcery and Cecelia or the Enchanted Chocolate Pot**. Harcourt, 2003, ©1988. 336p. $17. 978-0-15-204615-6. $7.99 Trade pb. 978-0-15-205300-0.
VOYA June 2003. **5Q · 5P · S · A/YA** (SF/F/H)
Best Books for Young Adults 2004.

Brought back into print and reminiscent in style of Jane Austen, this book consists of a correspondence between Kate and Cecelia. In reality, the two authors played the Letter Game, in which each takes on the persona of one of the characters. The first writer chooses the setting, time, and characters. Beginning the correspondence, Wrede becomes Cecelia, and Stevermer Kate. Kate is in London for her first "season," but her neighbor and best friend Cecelia has not been allowed to go. Missing each other dreadfully, they write to one another almost daily. Although the setting appears to be England during the Napoleonic Wars, there is a difference: Magic is prevalent-and legal. When Kate attends an investiture ceremony for Sir Hilary, one of their country neighbors, at the Royal College of Wizards, she stumbles into a small garden area and is bespelled by a frightening elderly woman. It turns out that this woman, Miranda, is an evil wizard who is trying to steal power from Thomas, marquis of Schofield. Kate and Cecelia become embroiled in the situation, attempting to prevent Miranda's success.

The plot is fairly complex as the two girls manage to get themselves into precarious situations (á la Lucy and Ethel, although the consequences here are much more dangerous). This is a fun story that quickly draws in the reader. The story will be more appreciated by teen girls than boys, and they will soon be requesting the sequel that is promised at the end of this book.—Marlyn Roberts.

Wright, Bil. **When the Black Girl Sings**. Simon & Schuster, 2007. 272p. $16.99. 978-1-4169-3995-5. $5.99 pb. 978-1-4169-4003-6.
VOYA February 2008. **5Q · 5P · M · J · S**

Quiet, naïve Lahni is having a tough year. Being the only African American in an exclusive all-girls' school in a suburb of New York City has always been a trial. The fact that her adoptive parents are white only adds to her challenge. When bad boy trouble and a potential divorce are added, the situation becomes almost more than she can handle. Her mother is struggling as well. She eventually drags Lahni with her to an interracial church where everything begins to fall into place for both of them. Lahni meets African American adults for the first time and finds out that it is okay to "use her own voice" both singing in the choir and dealing with her friends and family.

Without sugarcoating anything, Wright easily juggles the many issues found in the book with wit, compassion, and humor. The writing is clear, succinct, and never condescending. The main characters are shown as multifaceted people with strengths and weaknesses effectively adding to the authenticity of the book. Recommend this one to middle and high school girls who enjoy books about social situations and fitting in.—Angie Hammond.

Yep, Laurence. **City of Ice**. Starscape/Tor/Forge, 2011. 384p. $17.99. 978-0-7653-1925-8.

VOYA Online July 2011. **5Q · 5P · M · J · S**

For those who loved **City of Fire** (Tor, 2009/**VOYA** December 2009), book one of Yep's *City Trilogy*, this second volume will not disappoint. Set in 1941, this fast-moving fantasy adventure picks up mid-sky with twelve-year-old Scirye and her companions flying a magical wing to Nova Hafnia on the Arctic Circle. Her ragtag group of talented misfits (a tiny lap griffin, Kles; two street urchins, Leech and Koko; and the dragon Bayang) are still in pursuit of Mr. Roland who wants to collect the Five Lost Treasures of Emperor Yu. In this hazardous subzero territory of snow and ice, the group learns even mere survival can be a challenge. Thankfully, they find a friend and ally in Prince Tarkhun and his clever daughter, Roxanna. Roxanna and her ifrit servant bravely act as guides and interpreters for the troop as they follow the devious Mr. Roland and his evil dragon, Badik, to the treacherous Wastes land. It is largely due to the heroic efforts of Lord Resak, a gigantic polar bear, and his followers, that the band finally returns to Nova Hafnia-alive-but that is not the end. The nefarious Mr. Roland has stolen yet another Lost Treasure and continues on his quest for the rest. As in book one, Scirye has to appeal to the temperamental Spirit of the North whose capricious and unpredictable nature may make her more foe than friend.

The reader becomes immersed in the elaborately complex saga complete with its intriguing narrative and intricate characters. Yep has displayed his considerable skill in building a magnificent adventure, mixing both history and fantasy. The characters, who narrate alternating chapters in both volumes, are both strong and frail, heroic yet frightened, accountable and immature. This reader is looking forward to the final book in this most enjoyable trilogy.—Laura Canales.

Zafón, Carlos Ruiz. **The Prince of the Mists**. Little, Brown, 2010. 208p. $17.99. 978-0-316-04477-6. $8.99 Trade pb. 978-0-316-04480-6.

VOYA April 2010. **5Q · 5P · J · S**

When Max's dad convinces the family to move out of the city to a house on the ocean to escape World War II, the family is less than enthusiastic. The family grudgingly moves, but unfortunately, the house has secrets, as do the grounds, and Max and his sisters Alicia and Irina begin to experience odd events. Max can see an old graveyard from his window, and the mystery further deepens when he investigates and finds that the statues are not as they appear. After Irina falls down the stairs in a freak accident, Alicia and Max are left to fend for themselves. During one of their trips to town, Max meets Roland, the son of the lighthouse keeper. The three soon become friends, and Roland shows Max and Alicia the wreck of the Orpheus, a ship whose flag contains the same unusual symbol Max sees in the cemetery. As the skies darken and the ship resurfaces, will the three teens escape with their lives?

Zafon is a master storyteller. From the first page, the reader is drawn into the mystery and suspense that the young people encounter when they move into the Fleischmann house. The mists and the angry, stormy sea further add to the story's intensity. As the lighthouse keeper and his grandson's story is slowly revealed, the suspense becomes palpable. This book can be read and enjoyed by every level of reader, and teachers who are looking for a good read-aloud will keep the audience on the edge of their seats with this tale.—Lynn Evarts.

Zeises, Lara M. **Contents Under Pressure**. Delacorte, 2004. 256p. PLB $17.88. 978-0-385-90162-8.

VOYA June 2004. **5Q · 5P · M · J · S**

Lucy Doyle's life is changing. At fourteen, she feels left behind by her tight-knit group of middle school girlfriends, three of whom began seriously dating after graduation. Now Allison, her best friend since kindergarten, confesses a crush on Brad Thomas who liked Lucy last year. Jack, her brother and advisor, moved to college two years ago, and they have not spoken since school opened. With homecoming next weekend and Halloween in two weeks, Lucy feels stuck in a middle school rut—flat chested and never been kissed—behind her maturing friends. Lucy experiences six whirlwind weeks during which Jack moves home to think, bringing his pregnant girlfriend Hannah, whom Lucy dislikes but gains as a roommate. And then Lucy literally collides-three times-with the most sought-after junior boy, Tobin Scacheri, and winds up as his girlfriend. A series of significant talks help her to figure out her complicated world. Sex is often mentioned but never seen, and both Mom's and Hannah's advice on setting boundaries help Lucy approach Tobin to define their still-chaste comfort zone.

Fast-paced and funny, Zeises's engrossing book carries readers through a gamut of emotions while providing strong female role models. Every middle and junior high school girl and even some boys will want to read this novel. Librarians, parents, and classroom teachers in grades seven through ten should stock up on it.—Cynthia Winfield.

Zevin, Gabrielle. **Memoirs of a Teenage Amnesiac**. Farrar Straus Giroux, 2007. 288p. $17. 978-0-374-34946-2. $8.99 Trade pb. 978-0-312-56128-4.

VOYA October 2007. **5Q · 5P · J · S** (SF/F/H)

Best Books for Young Adults 2008.

When Naomi Porter realizes that she and Will Landsman, her best friend and co-editor of the yearbook, left a brand new $3,600 camera in the yearbook staff offices, they toss a coin to see who will make the trek from the school parking lot to the offices and back. Naomi loses the coin toss, and while she is walking back down the front steps of the school, she slips and falls. In desperation, she dives to save the camera. The camera survives intact, but Naomi does not. She hits her head on the steps and wakes up in an ambulance next to James Larkin, who claims to be her boyfriend. Naomi has no recollection of meeting James, nor of anything else that has happened in the last five years. Her friends and family are eager to help her get back to her life, but she is not certain that she wants to go back to being the person that everybody tells her she is.

The everyday events of Naomi's life appear to be standard-issue, young-adult-novel fare but Zevin takes romance, changing friendships, and familial dysfunctions and blends them with themes of chance, loss, and choice. The result is a quiet exploration of identity and self-realization that is simultaneously thought provoking and entertaining. Subtle humor helps to balance the abundance of serious themes. Peripheral characters are quirky and endearing, and Naomi is someone whom readers will love, hate, and want to be. This book will generate discussion and pass from teen to teen.—Carlisle K. Webber.

Title Index

Genre Index

Fantasy

Historical Fiction

Grade Level Interest

J Junior High (defined as grades 7-9).

S Senior High (defined as grades 10-12).

A/YA Adult-marketed book recommended for teens.

CPSIA information can be obtained at www.ICGtesting.com
Printed in the USA
BVOW06s1053180913

331399BV00002B/2/P